# UNITED STATES-LATIN AMERICA: A SPECIAL RELATIONSHIP?

# AEI-Hoover
policy studies

The studies in this series are issued jointly
by the American Enterprise Institute
for Public Policy Research and the Hoover
Institution on War, Revolution and Peace.
They are designed to focus on
policy problems of current and future interest,
to set forth the factors underlying
these problems and to evaluate
courses of action available to policy makers.
The views expressed in these studies
are those of the authors and do not necessarily
reflect the views of the staff, officers,
or members of the governing boards of
AEI or the Hoover Institution.

# UNITED STATES-
# LATIN AMERICA:
# A SPECIAL RELATIONSHIP?

Edmund Gaspar

American Enterprise Institute for Public Policy Research
Washington, D.C.

Hoover Institution on War, Revolution and Peace
Stanford University, Stanford, California

AEI-Hoover policy studies 26

**Library of Congress Cataloging in Publication Data**

Gaspar, Edmund.
    United States, Latin America, a special relationship?

    (AEI-Hoover policy studies ; 26) (Hoover Institution studies ; 63)
    1.   Latin America—Foreign relations—United States.
2.  United States—Foreign relations—Latin America.
3.  Pan-Americanism.  I.  Title.  II.  Series.
III.   Series: Hoover Institution studies ; 63.
F1418.G26        327.73'08        78-3533
ISBN 0-8447-3287-7

© 1978 by American Enterprise Institute for Public Policy Research, Washington, D.C. Permission to quote from or to reproduce materials in this publication is granted when due acknowledgment is made.

*Printed in the United States of America*

# Contents

INTRODUCTION ............................................. 1

## 1 THE SPIRITUAL CLEAVAGE BETWEEN TWO CIVILIZATIONS .......................... 5

The Hispano-Lusitanian Institutional Heritage  5
"Ariel versus Caliban"—A Latin American Diagnosis of the "Yankee Ills"  10
The Chances of a Spiritual Convergence  13

## 2 THE POLITICAL CONFLICT ..................... 17

The Roots of Dissent  17
The Age of Imperialism  19
The Idea of a United Western Hemisphere  22
The Monroe Doctrine  26

## 3 THE ECONOMIC CONFLICT ..................... 33

The Historical Background  33
An End to the Vicious Circles of Underdevelopment?  36
The Economic Bondage of Latin America  46
The Alliance for Progress  56

## 4 AMERICAN DIPLOMACY IN LATIN AMERICA .... 63

Personality and Role of the U.S. Envoy  63
The Inter-American System  67
The Options of U.S. Policy Making  77
The Panama Canal Treaties of September 1977  83
The Special Relationship Concept  89

# Introduction

In historical perspective the crisis of the inter-American system marks the climax of a long-simmering conflict between two civilizations. Although the Americas are related by the common Indo-European origin of their civilizations, North and South developed distinct patterns of life and different government systems. Their disagreements, dating back to their independence, have been perfunctorily papered over since then with instruments of international cooperation. This book is an attempt to get to the roots of their conflicts and gauge their depth and significance. It is the author's belief that distinguishing the real causes of disunity from the spurious ones will result in broader grounds for cooperation rather than trenches of division.

In a sense, the U.S.-Latin American dissension forms part of a worldwide rift between industrialized and developing nations, between the advanced First World and the backward Third and Fourth Worlds. Yet in the general spectrum of North-South polarization, Latin America might claim a special rank; for the Latin American republics are not divided by tribal heterogeneity, as are most African states. Nor do their populations cling to the ancient religious values and mores that hinder the socioeconomic development of some major Asian nations. On the contrary, Latin America shares with the United States a common Judeo-Christian and Greco-Roman cultural heritage, and a belief in the ideals of the French Revolution. When they became independent, the Latin American nations patterned their constitutions on that of the United States; and while they have violated the principles of democracy a thousand times, they have never ceased to pay lip service to them.

Until the early 1960s little had been heard in the outside world about Latin America's uncertainty concerning its position in the spectrum of world civilizations. Its peoples proudly considered themselves Westerners; their republics formed part of the Western economic and defense system, and some of them had been allies of the United States in World War II; and their special relationship with their northern neighbor was codified in the charter of the Pan American Union (now the Organization of American States), the first regional organization in the modern world. The peaceful solutions of inter-American conflicts have long served as models of impeccable international peace-making machinery. Thanks to the inter-American system, armed conflicts between members could be contained, and none evolved into the large-scale holocausts that twice in this century have ravaged the European continent.

Both North and South America belong to what is somewhat inaccurately designated as the Western cultural sphere, but they are two distinct branches of it. The countries to the north of the Rio Grande form part of the Anglo-Saxon family of nations, while those to the south are Latin—though this adjective was inexact even before a group of former British colonies with a cultural veneer of anglicism joined the inter-American system. We will nevertheless retain the adjective since there is no other word that so clearly describes the legacy of its Iberian conquerors. It might be argued, however, that Iberian values, reflexes, and attitudes are only displayed by the elites in the hemisphere, and that if any continent-wide class warfare were to sweep these elites from power and change the institutional order, it would also destroy Latin America's Iberian character.

Class warfare is certainly within the realm of possibility. The area's radical elites regard the wars of independence as unfinished business, as having created independent states but having left the "pigmentocracy" of the rich white elites intact. White dominance applies of course to the Andean and Central American republics and to some extent to Brazil alone. In the southern cone of the continent there are no sizable Indian masses, while in Mexico a revolution in the 1900s gave political power to the mestizos. Mexico demonstrates that a social revolution combined with a struggle for emancipation on the part of the Indians and mestizos need not destroy the intrinsically Iberian character of society and policy in Latin America. Even if they are not of Portuguese or Spanish descent, the revolutionary elites are usually so profoundly marked by this legacy that their victory is not likely to change the cultural physiognomy of the area they conquer.

The Cuban revolution has so far not contradicted this assumption. Although extra-continental ideological influences have been at work there since 1959, in a singularly insulated environment, they have not wiped out the Latin character of Cuba's tropical socialism. It remains grafted on the personality of a Mediterranean *caudillo* whose methods of leadership differ little from those of his Hispanic predecessors.

In other words, at present and for some time to come, U.S. policy makers will have to face Latin American leaders with an Iberian educational background and an Iberian psyche. Despite its differences from the North American cultural heritage, however, this Iberian background is still so much closer to its Anglo-Saxon parallel than to the Russian or Asian temperament that it unites at the same time that it divides the two Americas. The unifying cultural factors are to be found in the depths of every cultured American's consciousness. We are all spiritual sons and daughters of Greece, Rome, and Christianity. The dividing factors are rooted in the different socioeconomic legacies that England and Spain, the two main colonizing powers, bequeathed to the Americas.

The snags in communication between Latin Americans and North Americans can be traced back to the isolation in which the Spaniards and Portuguese kept their colonies. But when colonial rule came to an end, first in the North and later in the South, the two Americas emerged as two different worlds that had apparently little in common. The North was united, strong, and rich, and it soon started on its meteoric career as a world power. The South was disunited and poor, and it perpetuated a sociopolitical system whose feudal aspects, strong elitism, and lack of stability provided little impetus for socioeconomic progress. These handicaps were highlighted by the political stability, sound social system, and economic progress of the United States. By the turn of the century, Latin Americans—the early colonizers of the Americas, the aristocrats of the New World—found themselves living in an economic colony and political satellite of their northern neighbor.

That the hurt pride of the Latin Americans might provoke hostile reactions was to be expected. Yet the idea that Latin America belongs to the Third World rather than to the West took time to mature. Its origins might be traced back to Juan Domingo Perón's "third road" between capitalism and socialism, but it was Fidel Castro who gave it transcendence and dynamism, spreading it to the rest of the region in the 1960s. The leftist elites have put it on their banner, the younger generation of intellectuals has lent it theoretical support by exalting Indo-American indigenous values, and it has even crept into the official vocabulary of some Latin American republics. Resentment at having become an economic colony of the United States has sparked the idea that Latin America should join the Third World; for there the Latin American republics would find themselves in an environment more backward than their own. They are more developed in their institutions, richer, and technologically more advanced than most African and Asian states, and these qualities confer on them the ability to lead their less well-endowed Third World brethren. Fidel Castro seems to have proved this point by placing the superior organizational and technological know-how of his armed forces at the service of the leftist movement in Angola, helping it to victory and enhancing the prestige of Cuba in the Black Continent.

Not all the nations of the developing world are poor, however. The oil producing countries among them belong to the richest on the globe; for instance, oil deposits in Venezuela and Ecuador and unexpectedly rich reserves in Mexico have made it possible for these nations to ride the crest of the wave of nationalism in Latin America. The importance of the oil producing and oil exporting countries goes beyond the immediate objective of keeping oil prices high. Their organization, OPEC, is a successful experiment that may lead to the formation of similar cartels to control other Latin American food and raw material exports that are of vital importance to the United States.

The Latin American nations have obviously reached a crossroads where they must choose between their affective cultural and economic bonds with the West and the magnetism of a leading role in the Third World. Here is the crux of the crisis of the inter-American system, which is the theme of this book. Latin America is now searching for a new identity, and there are two elements that unite its nations in this quest—the predominance of Iberian values in their culture and political institutions, and the emotional opposition to the hegemony of the United States. Experience shows that while the Latin American governments are bitterly antagonistic toward each other on a great number of issues, they display a surprising unity whenever a confrontation with the United States arises. It would seem to follow that bipolarization of the Western Hemisphere is unavoidable at this stage, but history is not a logical process. It can be influenced by human ability. The lines of separation between the United States and Latin America are not yet sharply drawn, and many of the old ties that have linked the two parts of the Americas for over a century survive. It is up to American diplomacy to nurture these ties and create new links. Whether the borders that now separate the United States from its southern neighbors will become frontiers of hostility or gates to communication and friendship will depend, to a great extent, on the skill and sophistication of U.S. policy making.

# 1
# The Spiritual Cleavage between Two Civilizations

*The* ad-hoc *tendency of our decision-makers [in foreign policy] ... produces a relatively low valuation of historical factors. Nations are treated as similar phenomena, and those states presenting similar immediate problems are treated similarly. ... Great weight is given to what people say and relatively little to the significance of these affirmations in terms of domestic structure or historical background.*
                                                                HENRY A. KISSINGER[1]

### The Hispano-Lusitanian Institutional Heritage

Latin America is a graphic example of how vigorously ancestral structures can survive in the twentieth century. In remote jungle areas and on the inaccessible heights of the Andean high plateau, Indian tribes have conserved their stone-age or medieval ways of life. And where the lines of demarcation of Western civilization are drawn, they reflect the imprint of the Iberian conquerors. The strength of this heritage varies, of course, from country to country and from area to area depending on the degree of isolation from the outside world and the scope of immigration from Europe. Yet the institutional order left by Spain and Portugal has proved remarkably resistant to the erosion of time. It seems that Latin America, like its European mother countries, Spain and Portugal, is marked by an excess of institutional stability. Its apparent instability—the cavalcade of palace revolts that have marred its history—is a misleading semblance of change that hardly disturbs its deep-rooted structural rigidity.

The historic contribution of Spain and Portugal in extending Christian civilization to the New World must not be underestimated. They built beautiful cities and erected majestic cathedrals; they dotted the area with universities that have produced and are still producing

---

[1] *American Foreign Policy, Three Essays* (New York: W.H. Norton & Co., 1969), p. 33.

generations of brilliant intellectuals; they gave their colonies men who led the way in architecture, the creative arts, literature, and statesmanship; they imbued their progeny with a strong faith in God and a respect for human dignity; and they created widely different and better conditions for the integration of races than those that exist in the United States.

But they also carried out the colonization of the Americas in a different age, with different people and using methods that differed from those employed by England a century later. The pattern of conquest and colonization was by no means the same in North and South. In the English colonies the Anglo-Saxon enclave was limited and protected by the Appalachian barrier, which permitted consolidation of the settlements into a geopolitically cohesive area. Thus, the English colonies in North America grew organically from rural settlements into a larger but quite homogeneous political body that ultimately gave birth to a new nation.

In the South the conquest was carried out in zig-zags prompted by the search for treasure. From steppingstones in the Caribbean, the Spanish conquerors assaulted the highlands of Mexico to the north and the Pacific coast to the south, leaving large areas on the Atlantic shore and its hinterland unexplored and unoccupied. The gravitation to Mexico, Peru, and Paraguay, where the relatively civilized and docile indigenous populations provided the conquerors with cheap manpower, foreshadowed the dismemberment of the Spanish empire into independent units. A firm inner core of settlements like those in New England never came into being. The "disunited nations of America" were in a way a product of the conquest.

In further contrast to the pattern of colonization in the North, the Iberian conquerors transplanted into the New World their traditional preference for living in cities rather than in the countryside. This is one of the legacies of eight centuries of war against the Moors, during which the fortified town was a refuge against invaders. But concentrating the settlers in the cities prevented the development of rural areas and perpetuated a contrast between thriving cities and dreary villages languishing in ancestral apathy.[2]

---

[2] For a history of the conquest, see Salvador de Madariaga, *The Rise of the Spanish American Empire* (New York: Macmillan Co., 1965); Leopoldo Benítez Vinueza, *Ecuador, drama y paradoja* (Mexico: Fondo de Cultura Económica, 1950); Lewis Hanke, *The Spanish Struggle for Justice in the Conquest of America* (Philadelphia: University of Pennsylvania Press, 1949); Francisco López de Gamarra, *Cortés, the Life of the Conqueror by His Secretary* (Berkeley and Los Angeles: University of California Press, 1966); Rafael Altamira y Crevea, *La huella de España en América* (Madrid: Editorial Reus, 1924); and Ramón

The Hispanic conquerors institutionalized their rule over the native masses by imposing a specific form of serfdom attached to the *encomienda*. Each Spaniard was assigned by royal decree a huge tract of land together with the Indians living on it, whom he was entitled to use as serfs. When this form of exploitation wiped out the population of Hispaniola (the present Haiti and Dominican Republic), the court of Madrid gradually transformed it into a tributary system. The Indians were thenceforth taxed by the *encomendero*, but no longer required to render service to him; from a feudal landed property the *encomienda* evolved into a branch of the royal administration, and in the process the *encomendero* became a hereditary civil servant. Thus the *encomienda* contributed greatly to the development of an aristocracy without titles, to which many families of the present "oligarchy" in Latin America trace their origin. It became part of the psyche of the white man in Ibero-America. The prestige of the *encomenderos* and the power of the Spanish government agents surrounded civil service with an aura. *Empleomania*, the Latin American's obsession with working for the state—an employment that he considers safe, comfortable, and glamorous—is to a great extent a historical product of the institutionalization of the conquerors' privileges in the *encomienda*. Economic activity, industry, and commerce were despised by the proud descendants of the hidalgos. Mining served only the quick exploitation of the continent's gold and silver reserves, in a rapine, early capitalist approach to natural resources and manpower.

The difficult communication between the motherland and the colonies resulted in a long lapse of time between the enactment of royal legislation in Spain and its implementation overseas. The court in Madrid tried to impose its will through a complex and highly centralized administrative apparatus and a system of checks and counter-checks. But its overseas representatives soon succeeded in reconciling the royal will with their own wishes; the law was respected but not

---

Menéndez Pidal, *El Padre Las Casas, su doble personalidad* (Madrid: Espasa-Calpe, 1963).

On the racial and cultural elements in Latin America, see Magnus Mörmer, *Race Mixture in the History of Latin America* (Boston: Little, Brown & Co., 1967); William Lytle Schurz, *This New World, the Civilization of Latin America* (New York: E.P. Dutton & Co., 1964); Frank MacShane, ed., *Impressions of Latin America—Five Centuries of Travel and Adventure by English and American Writers* (New York: William Morrow & Co., 1963); Fernando Guillén Martinez, *La torre y la plaza, un ensayo de interpretación de América* (Madrid: Ediciones Cultura Hispánica, 1958); Gilberto Freyre, *The Masters and Slaves* (New York: Alfred A. Knopf, 1967); Germán Arciniegas, *Latin America, A Cultural History* (New York: Alfred A. Knopf, 1967); and Angel Rosenblat, *La población indígena y el mestizaje en América*, vols. 1, 2 (Buenos Aires: Editorial Nova, 1954).

obeyed. The paradox *obedecemos pero no cumplimos* (we obey but we do not comply) reflects a pattern of behavior that characterized Spain's overseas possessions from the very outset of colonization.[3]

A comprehensive analysis of the sociocultural differences between North and South America should not ignore the fact that the Iberian colonizers were Catholic and those of the North predominantly Protestant. Aside from theological and ritual differences, this implied a different ethical attitude toward civic duties; among Spanish Catholics a tendency developed not to consider it a sin to neglect one's duty toward the state. According to contemporary records, even priests did not consider smuggling morally wrong.

Owing to the rigid trade regulations established by the Spanish crown, smuggling became the only way to keep open the channels of commerce between the Spanish possessions in the Americas and the outside world, and contraband is still a drain on the national economies of Latin America. Although it flouts customs barriers and foments inflation, it also points up the need for freer circulation of merchandise in an area nowadays divided into multiple national units. On the whole, however, smuggling is still not considered disreputable by the average Latin American. And since one violation may entail others, it is like a fissure in a wall that weakens the entire structure.

But smuggling is not the only surviving example of disregard of the law. The Crown's humanitarian legislation to protect the exploited natives became another source of abuse. The Iberian legal mind was sophisticated enough to find loopholes through which the benefits extended to the Indians by the royal administration were vitiated by its colonial agents. "We obey but we do not comply" reflects the latent spirit of revolt that simmered in the colonies long before the wars of independence began in the nineteenth century; and habits make mores. Generations of citizens grew up in the New World in a tradition that considered evasion of the law an accepted routine, a necessary mechanism through which to elude rules imposed by a distant foreign government and regarded as impracticable under the specific circumstances existing in the colonies. And this psychology boomeranged when the provinces won their independence from the Spanish Crown.

---

[3] On the Spanish colonial institutions, see C. H. Haring, *The Spanish Empire in America* (New York: Harcourt, Brace & World, 1963); Silvio Zavala, *La encomienda indiana* (Madrid: Junta de Relaciones Culturales del Ministerio del Estado, 1935); Hubert Herring, *A History of Latin America* (New York: Harcourt, Brace & World, 1963); Salvador de Madariaga, *El ocaso del imperio español en América* (Buenos Aires: Editorial Sudamericana, 1959); J. H. Parry, *The Spanish Seaborne Empire* (London: Hutchinson & Co., 1966); and Francisco José Moreón, *Legitimacy and Stability in Latin America* (New York: New York University Press, 1969).

Many Latin American republics have promulgated laws and adopted constitutions that rival those of even the most progressive Western nations, while maintaining a degree of corruption, misery, and oppression comparable to that of an Eastern satrapy.[4]

As Spanish Catholicism took a dim view of civic duties, so it underrated the importance of other wordly activities. The medieval idea that the business of earning one's daily bread was less important than earning eternal salvation was firmly rooted in the Spanish mentality. The Church preached that worldly business should be limited strictly to providing oneself with a livelihood compatible with one's social rank, leaving enough time to attend to the paramount business of saving one's soul. How far this doctrine was meant for the consumption of the impoverished masses and cynically disregarded by the colonial ruler and the Catholic hierarchy is open to discussion, but it is evident that this kind of philosophy was less conducive to great material achievement than was the Protestant ethic of the Anglo-Saxon settlers.[5] The latter inherited from England a class system based on differences in wealth; they believed that wealth was a blessing from God. Both ideas came to be rejected by the Latin American intelligentsia as utterly materialistic and antithetic to the humanistic values of the Iberian cultural heritage.

---

[4] On postcolonial political systems and social structures, see Bartolomé Mitre, *Historia de San Martín y de la emancipación sud americana*, 4 vols. (Buenos Aires: Editorial Felix Lajouane, 1889–1890); Jacques Lambert, *Latin America, Social Structures and Political Institutions*, trans. H. Katel (Berkeley and Los Angeles: University of California Press, 1971); Seymour Martin Lipset and Aldo Solari, eds., *Elites in Latin America* (New York: Oxford University Press, 1967); Orlando Fals Borda, *Subversion and Social Change in Colombia*, trans. D. Skiles (New York: Columbia University Press, 1969); James Petras, *Politics and Social Forces in Chilean Development* (Berkeley and Los Angeles: University of California Press, 1970); Eduardo Santa, *Sociología política de Colombia* (Bogotá: Ediciones Tercer Mundo, 1964); Russell H. Fitzgibbon, *Uruguay, Portrait of a Democracy* (London: George Allen & Unwin, 1956); Claudio Véliz, "Centralism and Nationalism in Latin America," *Foreign Affairs* (October 1968), pp. 69 ff; and Lucian W. Pye, "The Non-Western Political Process," *The Journal of Politics*, vol. 20 (1958).

[5] On the role of the Catholic Church in Latin America, see Ivan Vallier, "Religious Elites," in *Elites in Latin America*, ed. Lipset and Solari (New York: Oxford University Press, 1967); Francois Houtart and Emile Pin, S. J., *The Church and the Latin American Revolution* (New York: Sheed & Ward, 1965); Frederick B. Pike, ed., *The Conflict Between Church and State in Latin America* (New York: Alfred A. Knopf, 1964); Emile Pin, S. J., *Elementos para una sociología del catolicismo latinoamericano* (Fribourg, Switzerland and Bogotá, Colombia: Feres, 1963); Thomas C. Bruneau, *The Political Transformation of the Brazilian Catholic Church* (New York: Cambridge University Press, 1974); Ivan Vallier, *Catholicism, Social Control and Modernization in Latin America* (Englewood Cliffs: Prentice Hall, 1970); and Brian H. Smith, S. J., "Religion and Social Change: Classical Theories and New Formulations in the Context of Recent Developments in Latin America," *Latin American Research Review*, vol. 10, no. 2 (Summer 1975), pp. 3-34.

The pioneer of North America was a product of early capitalistic development in England. The Spanish conquistador had no such experience. He brought with him the military values of the hidalgo and his contempt for physical labor and business.

Thus, the society that the conquerors built still juxtaposes material and spiritual paradoxes. Amidst infinite misery and insolent wealth, it preserves a refined concept of human dignity and a contemptuous disregard for material welfare. It perpetuates the centralistic structure of the Spanish administration in the empire's successor states. It keeps alive the Mediterranean propensity to evade the law while paying lip service to it. The feudalism it built developed a devotion to civil service without paving the way toward democratic decentralization, as the European feudal systems had done.

The Balkanization of the Spanish colonial empire did not destroy its cultural cohesion. The colonial legacy is perceptible—mutatis mutandis—in the institutions and mores of all Latin American republics. Thus, in order to properly evaluate the Latin American political process, one must make a thorough analysis of its colonial ingredients. The virtues and sins of the conquerors are integral parts of it, as are the character and culture of the natives.

Even revolutionary ideologies transplanted to Latin American soil are bent to conform with the deeply ingrained attitudes of the local psyche. The conquerors managed to accommodate their visionary utopias to the cosmic realities of the soil by using the same mental acrobatics that enabled them to gloss over such of the strictures of monarch and Church as they deemed inapplicable.

### "Ariel versus Caliban"—A Latin American Diagnosis of the "Yankee Ills"

By the turn of this century the Latin American intelligentsia had come to grips with the idea that their republics had been left behind in the worldwide race for wealth and had become politically and economically dependent on the colossus of the North. They have since tried to find consolation in an elitist philosophy that underrates the cultural achievements of the United States and exalts their own values.

Few Latin American writers exerted as much influence upon the thinking of his contemporaries as did the Uruguayan José Enrique Rodó in his brilliant essay *Ariel*, first published in 1900.[6] The thoughts expressed in *Ariel* are still remarkably topical, and the essay is counted

---

[6] See José Enrique Rodó, *Ariel*, trans. G. Brotherston (New York: Cambridge University Press, 1967).

as a catalog of "Yankee Ills" by many of today's intellectuals in Latin America. Ariel, based on the character in Shakespeare's *The Tempest,* symbolizes the airy spirit of culture, and is contrasted with Caliban, the coarse embodiment of materialism. Although Rodó did not specify that Ariel symbolized the South and Caliban the North, the two Shakespearean characters became synonymous with the North-South antithesis.

Rodó saw in the English aristocracy the most perfect embodiment of a superior way of life since the era of the Greek city-states. He noted that in the United States, on the contrary, there was no social class to prevent the rise of vulgarity. The laudable efforts of the North Americans to popularize general education neither improved their low aesthetic standards, nor helped even the most talented to transcend mediocrity. Their war against ignorance resulted in universal semi-civilization and a stagnation of culture on the higher levels.

Rodó was also opposed to the kind of mass democracy advocated at that time by the North Americans. In *Ariel*, he claimed that government should not be surrendered into the hands of an uncivilized majority. Democracy would lead civilization to lose in depth what it had gained in breadth. And this danger, he wrote, was particularly imminent in America, where the young and relatively feeble national groups, lacking the political stability and the firm cultural roots of the older nations, might be unable to assimilate cosmopolitan masses of immigrants. He was deeply concerned lest admiration for North American material achievements gain ground in Latin America, thereby delatinizing the area by stripping it of its ethnic and cultural heritage.

The North Americans' passion for work and stubborn insistence on material progress could only be acceptable, in Rodó's opinion, if this materialism represented a preliminary stage in their culture. In fact, however, their utilitarianism was irreconcilable with their religious beliefs. Success as an end in itself sharply contradicted the ideas expressed in Thomas à Kempis's *Imitation of Christ*, and unfortunately, said Rodó, one did not find in the depth of the North American psyche anything that foretold a change in this respect.

The poetic springs of the English mind dried up in the fever of conquest and commerce. Utilitarianism penetrated public administration, and democracy was unable to uproot corruption. The rule of the majority was checked in the worst possible way by a plutocracy reminiscent of the Roman republic in the later years, when the predominance of a wealthy and arrogant upper class heralded the decline of democracy and paved the way for the tyranny of the Caesars. In North America the man of the newly conquered West took the place of the Virginian or the Yankee as the representative of Americanism. Chicago came to dominate Boston and Philadelphia, claiming superiority over the Atlantic seaboard by arguing that the latter was too reactionary, too European, and too traditionalist.

North Americans, intoxicated by their prosperity, continued Rodó, had tried to propagate their system. They were convinced that their contributions to the ideals of freedom and material progress required shifting the axis of the world to North America; and they considered their formula—George Washington plus Thomas Edison—to be the equivalent of all the achievements of European Aryans, from ancient Greece to today.

But North Americans did not have the character to qualify them for hegemony. With no talent for propaganda, no vocation of apostle, and lacking both charm and urbanity, they could not make their civilization as attractive as that of Greece, in which all people believed they could find something of their own personality.

Although many of its findings are outdated, Rodó's *Ariel* remains an important bulwark of intellectual anti-U.S. bias in Latin America. Of course he borrowed freely from contemporary European writers like Renan, Bourget, Fouillée, Carlyle, Taine, and others. He looked on the northern upstarts with the jaundiced eye of a descendant of the oldest of European civilizations. He was by no means alone in snubbing this new type of North American who personified the rise of Chicago over the traditionally intellectual eastern cities. Many leading Latin Americans reacted in similar fashion to the success story of the North, their attitude being that of an impoverished aristocrat toward his rich, parvenu neighbor. Rodó's writing reflects a mental colonialism fascinated by Europe, which has been disavowed by some modern Latin American intellectuals but which still constitutes the mental framework of important sectors of the area's intelligentsia.

In most of his predictions, Rodó proved a rather shortsighted prophet. It was not in the North but in the South that bureaucratic venality and plutocratic pressure brought about the "tyranny of Caesar." He was also wrong in considering North American society unable to produce an intellectual elite and a sophisticated culture. On the whole, Rodó and his school seem to have overestimated the effectiveness of an elite-oriented cultural development and underestimated the solidity of North America's mass culture and mass democracy. The concept of a small, educated, and refined elite class serving as the focal point for a national culture has not always been realized even in Europe, where the traditional elites have had a more established influence on mass civilization than those of Latin America. The elite-oriented patterns of other civilizations have failed to penetrate the masses in Asia, the former European colonies of Africa, and to a great extent also Latin America.

One of Rodó's observations, however, could hardly be questioned—that North Americans failed to project an image of themselves that would truly reflect the intrinsic values of their philosophy and way of life. Hollywood films have rendered an ambiguous service to the image of the United States in the world. While their popularity in Latin America has spread U.S. habits and mannerisms throughout the continent, they have also aroused envy of that country's wealth in the masses and provoked criticism of its way of life among the intelligentsia.

That Rodó and his followers nourished certain illusions is another matter. He dreamed of converting all American society, in both North and South, into a haven not only for immigrant masses but also for certain redeeming ideas. He hoped that Ariel, "that symbol of reason and delicate sentiment," would triumph over Caliban, that rebel of low instincts. He thought the triumph of Ariel would mean the rule of ideals and order in life, noble inspiration in thinking, altruism in morals, refined taste in the arts, heroism in action, and delicacy in manners. How far his dreams may become reality one day through a convergence of North and South American ideas is the subject of the next section of this study.

### The Chances of a Spiritual Convergence

For most North Americans the Latin American way of life and Latin American institutions are so perplexing, so alien, that they perceive only the ills thereof, overlooking their good qualities. They are shocked by the extravagance of a world that differs basically from their own. They abhor the abyss that separates the rich from the poor. They are puzzled by the contrast between booming cities with showpiece modern architecture and the shantytowns around them. They are appalled by the dichotomy between democratic rhetoric and autocratic government practices. They are baffled by the fact that religion is more a habit of adherence to certain rituals than a moral and intellectual commitment to Christian dogma. They view machismo as an ugly double standard in favor of men, and their egalitarian philosophy is scandalized by the male chauvinism of Latin American men. But nothing disturbs them as much as the hostility they so often meet in Latin American countries where the Yankee is sometimes regarded as the source of all the ills that beset the area.

This culture shock blurs the vision of North Americans, and they fail to see the positive aspects of life in Latin America. They often do not realize that tyranny and the disparities between social classes are corollaries of the intensely dramatic history of Latin Americans—something the more fortunate North Americans have never experienced. They do not perceive that the closely knit Latin American family is more stable and cohesive than the Anglo-Saxon family. They ignore the fact that communication between Latin Americans is easier and more spontaneous, and that therefore alienation is less frequent than among Anglo-Saxons, or that rhetoric often serves as an outlet for passions under the surface. They fail to notice that the principles of Catholicism, although apparently disowned and neglected, are at work in the subconscious of every Latin American, including those who profess to be atheists. Even North American sociologists do not realize that there is a robust and powerful Latin American middle class whose strength must be measured not by income brackets but by cultural and moral standards.

North American criticism of the hypocrisy of Latin American rulers, who preach democracy and practice dictatorship, misses the point that such behavior represents an accommodation to the historical conditions of statesmanship, that the dictatorships are bridging the inherent contradiction between anarchism and authoritarianism in the Iberian mind without resorting to totalitarian methods. When North Americans claim that Latin Americans are insensitive to the ills of their society, they forget that their southern neighbors are more open to the horizons of the world than the more parochial Anglo-Saxons, and that racial discrimination has been less aggressive in Latin America than in the United States.

Such a negative vision of Latin America, juxtaposed to the equally negative approach of the Latin Americans to North American values, seems to contravene the possibility of a rapprochement between the two mentalities. This, however, is a superficial prognosis. Latin America is now seeking a new identity[7] that must include some of the more valuable elements of Anglo-Saxon socioeconomic culture if the shocking backwardness that prevails there is to be overcome. But as this search for self-identification gains strength, the United States is losing its earlier complacency with regard to its system of values. It has paraded for decades on the world stage as the richest and most balanced society

---

[7] On the Latin American search for a new identity, see Victor Raúl Haya de la Torre, *Indoamerica* (Lima: Ediciones Pueblo, 1961); Eudocio Ravines, *América Latina, un Continente en erupción*, 2nd ed. (Buenos Aires: Ediciones Claridad, July 1956); Eudocio Ravines, *La gran promesa* (Madrid: Aguilar, 1963); Leopoldo Zea, *The Latin American Mind* (Norman: University of Oklahoma Press, February 1970); Harold Eugene Davis, ed., *Latin American Social Thought*, 2nd ed. (Washington, D.C.: The University Press of Washington, 1966); Daniel Cosío Villegas, *American Extremes* (Austin: University of Texas Press, 1964); and Francisco José Moreno, *Legitimacy and Stability in Latin America, A Study of Chilean Political Culture* (New York: New York University Press, 1969).

mankind has known, but today large segments of its population are claiming that they have been pariahs in that society. It has been brought to public notice that there are millions of blacks, poor Appalachian whites, and others who are jobless or underemployed and are living a marginal life at or even below subsistence level. Publicity about these deficiencies has dealt a tremendous blow to the prestige of the United States. It has destroyed its image as an efficient resolver of socioeconomic problems. It has cast a shadow of doubt on the praiseworthiness of the American consumer society as a whole, and the radical wing of American youth has come to the conclusion that the fetishism of material values is an iniquity that must be wiped out.

These bitter conclusions have also led to a lack of faith in U.S. foreign aid and technology as a universal panacea. North American policy makers have apparently been tempted by the idea that Latin Americans can be ushered into the twentieth century simply by offering them the same incentives that helped the industrial West to its present wealth and power. Rousseau's concept of the "noble savage," which to some degree inspired the North American Declaration of Independence, justified universal application of the North American system. The United States based its aid policies on the belief that any nation or any regional group could become prosperous, stable, and democratic by simply following its example.

When this idea was put into practical application in the Alliance for Progress, however, it failed, as we shall see later on. Ethnic communities that have lived together for centuries and developed a common set of cultural and ethical standards and a common pattern of behavior are infinitely more reluctant to assimilate North American values than the individual immigrants to the United States. The success of the North American melting pot might easily lead to erroneous conclusions.

**Rapprochement in the realm of ideas** must be sought elsewhere. As a first condition of this search, the simplistic vision of other nations as potential beneficiaries of the North American heritage should be abandoned. It is a vision that derives from an egocentric concept of the world. It assumes the existence of a universal remedy for the ills of mankind and suggests that the ills of any given society are those that have been branded so by the Puritan Anglo-Saxon legacy.

But to qualify for full partnership with the industrial world, our neighbors to the South will also have to renounce some of their elitist, idealistic concepts of life, which—paradoxically—coexist with a rapine, capitalist mentality. A meeting ground between the two civilizations postulates a similarly balanced approach to intellectual and material values. North Americans are indeed on the verge of reevaluating their materialistic inheritance in favor of a greater appreciation of cultural values; but before a balance between North and South America can be struck, the latter must resolve its more dramatic socioeconomic problems.

Convergence of the two civilizations is not impossible, but it will take a long time. It may come about through a reappraisal of both areas' cultural legacies and a more balanced relationship in terms of wealth and power. At present, North American policy makers must take into account the realities of a *bipolar* Western Hemisphere.

# 2
# The Political Conflict

*We have no concern with South America: we have no sympathy, we can have no well-founded political sympathy with them. We are sprung from different stocks, we speak different languages, we have been brought up in different social and moral schools, we have been governed by different codes of law, we profess radically different forms of religion.*
The North American Review and<br>Miscellaneous Journal[1]

*Our experience with your country [the United States] cannot be compared to those of other nations which lived and survived in the ominous shadow of implacable imperialisms.*
ALBERTO LLERAS CAMARGO[2]

### The Roots of Dissent

The first contacts between England and the closed world of the Spanish and Portuguese overseas possessions were the incursions of English buccaneers into the Spanish colonies of the Caribbean. The raids of pirates like Drake, Hawkins, and Morgan spread destruction and death in the flourishing Spanish towns of Santo Domingo, Panama, and Cartagena. They acted with the tacit consent of the English Crown, serving as spearheads for British expansion into the West Indies. On the other hand, cultural exchange between the Hispanic and Anglo-Saxon worlds did not develop in colonial times, owing to the hostility between Spain and England and the fact that Spanish Catholic dogmatists abhorred the British Protestant settlers as heretics. The Inquisition —usually more tolerant in its American outposts than in the mother country—proceeded mercilessly against any infiltration of heretic literature.

---

[1] Vol. 12 (Boston: 1821), cited by Lewis Hanke, *Do the Americas Have a Common History? A Critique of the Bolton Theory* (New York: Alfred A. Knopf, 1964).

[2] From a speech by the former Colombian president before the United States Congress, April 6, 1960.

The revolt of the North American colonists against Great Britain provided Spain with an opportunity to take revenge on a hereditary enemy. From the very outset of the North American revolution the Spanish governor of Louisiana extended aid in the form of ammunition and equipment to the Continental Army of General (Lighthorse Harry) Lee, and supported the activities of the U.S. Congress's agent in New Orleans, Oliver Pollack. In June 1779, Spain declared war on England. The talented young governor of New Orleans, Bernardo de Gálvez, who commanded a small Spanish force composed of mercenaries of varying nationality, social class, and color, waged a victorious small war against the British, taking by assault the fortresses of Baton Rouge, Mobile, and Pensacola. The Spanish campaign in Florida, which lifted British pressure from the southern flank of Washington's army, proved to be decisive in the victory of the insurgents.[3]

The gaining of independence by the United States had a profound impact on Hispanic America. Thenceforth, Spanish-American liberals looked upon their northern neighbor as being in the vanguard of their democratic ideals, a model to be imitated. But the United States was reluctant to accept the role of liberator or to promote a liberal revolution in Spanish America. The halfhearted aid given by the United States to Miranda's expedition, which sailed from New York harbor on February 2, 1806, and for whose tragic failure five North Americans also paid with their lives, represented the only exception to the universally cold reaction of the United States toward the revolts in the South. For those Latin Americans who pinned their hopes on North American help, U.S. neutrality came as a cold shower. As Simón Bolívar said: "We had hoped that all civilized nations would hurry to our help. . . . But how frustrated were our hopes! Not only Europeans but also our brothers to the north remained immobile spectators of this conflict."[4]

Apparently, the historical misunderstanding between the North and the South stems from their initial contacts after they emerged as independent *American* nations. Latin Americans expected the North to act in the spirit of the principles underlying the Declaration of Independence and to side with them in their fight for national independence and a republican form of government. The United States, however, reacted to the South's plea in a pragmatic, restrained manner; although

---

[3] See Buchanan Parker Thomson, *La ayuda española en la guerra de la independencia norteamericana*, trans. E. B. Crespo (Madrid: Ediciones Cultura Hispánica, 1967).

[4] Daniel Florencio O'Leary, *Bolívar y la emancipación de Sur-América*, transl. from English by Simon B. O. Leary and published in *Memorias del general O'Leary*, vol. 1 (Madrid: Biblioteca Ayacucho, 1915), p. 376.

the special envoys from the rebellious Spanish colonies were greeted with sympathy in the press, they met with coolness from the government. In 1815 the United States withdrew the consuls appointed earlier to some Latin American cities, and made it possible for Spain to purchase arms and ships. The first conflict between the United States and Latin America was sparked by Bolívar's confiscation of two North American ships carrying food and weapons to the defenders of the Spanish fort of Angostura. The protest lodged by U.S. representative Irvine with Bolívar on this issue gave rise to an acrimonious discussion during which the latter said that despite the terrible sacrifices imposed on Venezuela by the war against Spain, it was ready to fight the whole world if attacked.[5] U.S. policy makers were at that time absorbed by negotiations with Spain on the ceding of Florida,[6] and had little desire to strain relations with the Court of Madrid by abandoning the safe platform of strict neutrality vis-à-vis Spain and its colonies.

## The Age of Imperialism

The cleavage between realistic U.S. policy and the romantic illusions of the Latin Americans about the redemptory role of the United States in the world became manifest at independent Spanish America's first encounter with the independent United States. The northern giant, bent on pursuing its territorial expansion and protecting its own security, was to appear thenceforth to its turbulent southern neighbors as the policemen of the Hemisphere rather than as a partner with whom to work toward economic and social progress. The conquest of more than half of Mexico, the colonization of Puerto Rico, intervention in the Caribbean and Central America, and the creation of Panama as an independent republic were stages in a consistent great-power policy, not unlike that of the Western European states during the same period. The nineteenth century was the age of imperialism, led by Great Britain, which extended its rule over 21 million square miles of territory; France, whose colonial empire grew by 7.5 million square miles, and little Holland, which subjugated both the East and West Indies encompassing a densely populated area of 1.25 million square miles. The United States also entered the race, founding its own colonial empire

---

[5] On the wars of independence of the Spanish colonies, see Victor Andrés Belaúnde, *Bolívar y el pensamiento político de la revolución hispanoamericana* (Madrid: Ediciones Cultura Hispánica, 1959); Enrique Camposo Menéndez, *Se llamaba Bolívar*, 6th ed. (Santiago de Chile: Empresa Editora Zig-Zag, 1954); Salvador de Madariaga, *El ocaso del imperio español en América*, 2nd ed. (Buenos Aires: Editorial Sudamericana, 1959); and Parry, *Spanish Seaborne Empire*.
[6] Settled by the Florida Treaty of February 22, 1819.

that embraced Puerto Rico, the Panama Canal area, the Virgin Islands, and the Philippines—a total of roughly 200,000 square miles of territory, of which only 5,500 square miles were in the Western Hemisphere. Indeed, the United States carved for itself a rather modest slice of the enormous cake served up at the colonial banquet.[7]

The U.S. expansion on the North American continent differed from the classical pattern of overseas colonization. It can only be compared with the thrust of tsarist Russia into Siberia, Kirgizia, Turkestan, and the Caucasus, initiated in 1581 by the private expediton of a small detachment of Cossacks and escalated into the conquest of an area embracing 9.5 million square miles. There, as in the case of the U.S. expansion into the southwest, a young, dynamic state flexed its muscles, crushing the resistance of a less organized and militarily inferior enemy. In both cases, vast expanses of sparsely settled land were subdued with the long-range purpose of eventual settlement by the conqueror's population. The Russian process of expansion was slower than that of the United States, lasting almost 300 years, from the end of the sixteenth century to the end of the nineteenth century;[8] but it encompassed an area roughly seven times as large as that wrested from Mexico by the United States. It suppressed such historical states as Armenia and Georgia, and subjugated dozens of nationalities without the slightest prospect of assimilating them into the Russian ethnic body. In contrast to the relatively small problem of assimilating and acculturating the Spanish-Mexican ethnic elements into the main ethnic body of the United States, the various nationalities of the Soviet Union compose about half the total population, and were it not for the heavy-handed rule of Moscow they would threaten to tear apart the fabric of the Russian-dominated empire.

A hypothetical expansion of the same dimensions as that of Russia in Asia and the Caucasus by the United States would have brought the entire Western Hemisphere under the rule of Washington, and the Anglo-Saxon ethnic pivot of such an empire would have ultimately faced the same problems of adjustment that now confront the Soviet Union.

Within the massive body of arguments depicting the United States

---

[7] Some Latin American authors draw a parallel between manifest destiny and the philosophy of German imperialists—"the overseas rivals of the United States." This interpretation takes the American and German belief in racial supremacy as a common frame of reference. See E. Ramírez Novoa, *La política yanqui en América Latina*, vols. 1, 2 (Lima: Ediciones "28 de Julio", 1962), p. 34.

[8] Although Siberia was militarily occupied in the seventeenth century, mass colonization of it by peasant settlers was undertaken only at the end of the nineteenth century.

as the policeman of the hemisphere, the usurper of its resources, and the obstacle to its economic and social development, historical background plays a rather modest role. Yet those with an axe to grind bring into the context of recent U.S. policies the initial refusal of the U.S. government to lend effective help to the uprisings of its southern neighbors. Such writers use analogies which, although historically irrelevant, have the advantage of suggesting a monolithic U.S. body politic, always inspired by antipopular and antidemocratic thinking. They support their theory by citing historical examples, beginning with the refusal of the U.S. government to recognize the independence of Haiti[9] (the first American country after the United States to shake off colonial domination) and ending with U.S. intervention in the Dominican Republic in 1965. They claim that although U.S. imperialism may change its methods it never stops trying to gain control of markets, raw materials, navigation routes, and strategic bases from which to protect its commerce. They maintain that the United States intervenes militarily in order to eliminate another imperialistic rival; or it fosters domestic troubles in order to set up lackeys as rulers in certain Latin American countries, where these despots, in serving U.S. interests, thwart every possibility of establishing a democratic regime. The United States has made use of every available method or system of aggression to secure its economic hegemony.[10]

In the view of these historians, the Monroe Doctrine, the big stick of Theodore Roosevelt, the dollar diplomacy of Taft, the Good Neighbor Policy of Franklin Roosevelt, and the Alliance for Progress of John Kennedy are but different facets of the same striving for hegemony. The methods change, but the objective remains the same—to establish the United States as the center of a solar system, with its satellites, the "disunited states of Latin America," orbiting in the sphere of its military and economic supremacy.

The historical interpretation of U.S.-Latin American relations, which views the United States in the role of an imperialistic monster ready to devour its smaller sisters, or as a shark hunting small and defenseless sardines,[11] is obviously not the only version of Latin American thinking on the matter. There exist more balanced and historically more objective views, which set U.S. policy in its proper context. Unfortunately, such opinions are limited to a narrow sector of the Latin American intelligentsia. Emotional dislike of the United States, its

---

[9] The United States took into consideration the sentiments of the southern slaveholding states.
[10] Novoa, *La política yanqui*, p. 40.
[11] A reference to José Arévalo, *The Shark and the Sardines*, trans. J. Cobb and R. Osegueda (New York: L. Stuart, 1961).

policies, and its people runs like a thread among all political elements, from anarchists to national conservatives. It operates to unite government coalitions composed of the strangest political bedfellows. As Arthur P. Whitaker and David C. Jordan put it, "A major ingredient of Latin American nationalism in this century has unquestionably been anti-Americanism or Yankeephobia."[12] Its emotional impact is a windfall for the aspirations of international communism. In moments of crisis, Communist agitators try to kindle a revolution by appealing to the anti-imperialist feelings of the masses.

## The Idea of a United Western Hemisphere

The different patterns of colonization, the dissimilar temperaments of the men who settled North and South America, their divergent political orientation and religious beliefs, did not contribute to the formation of a hemispheric community spirit. The Spanish policy of isolating the colonies from any kind of extraneous influence, be it trade or cultural exchange, only deepened the cleavage between two worlds located in the same hemisphere but separated from each other by political as well as economic, cultural, and religious barriers. Yet isolation did not prevent the intelligentsia of the North from reading the "black legend," the vituperations of Fr. Bartolomé de Las Casas against the Spanish conquistadores. His lurid descriptions of Spanish cruelty, fanaticism, and greed for gold marked their thinking about their southern neighbors.[13]

The first intellectual communication between the Iberian and Anglo-Saxon worlds took the form of reports and literature about the North American revolution. These were read avidly and regarded by Latin American intellectuals either as marvelous messages of freedom or as ominous warnings that the era of aristocratic privilege might soon come to an end. Some democrats in theory but aristocrats by birth and temperament—such as one of the precursors of Latin American independence, General José Miranda—were shocked to see North American democracy at work and feared, like Rodó, almost a century later, the tyranny of the common people.[14]

---

[12] Arthur P. Whitaker and David C. Jordan, *Nationalism in Contemporary Latin America* (New York: The Free Press, 1966), p. 188.

On Latin American nationalism, see also Samuel L. Bailey, ed., *Nationalism in Latin America* (New York: Alfred A. Knopf, 1971), and Frederick C. Turner, *The Dynamic of Mexican Nationalism* (Chapel Hill: The University of North Carolina Press, 1968).

[13] Menéndez Pidal, *El Padre Las Casas*. The book is a somewhat biased plea for the cause of the Spanish colonizers and a strong indictment of Las Casas, whom Menéndez Pidal considers a "paranoiac."

[14] José de Onís, ed., *Los Estados Unidos vistos por escritores latinoamericanos* (Madrid: Ediciones Cultura Hispánica, 1956), pp. 97-98.

Yet after independence had been won by the Latin American republics the idea that the two halves of the Western Hemisphere shared a common destiny gradually gained ground in both the North and the South. George Washington referred to it in his farewell address; Thomas Jefferson and John Quincy Adams developed it into a broader concept of hemispheric isolationism; and James Monroe codified it in his message to Congress in 1823.

In the South, Simón Bolívar became the founder of Pan Americanism. His idea of hemispheric cooperation did not originally include the United States, probably out of fear that it would dominate the entire hemispheric structure. But as we shall see later, he ultimately invited the United States to the first Pan American Conference in Panama in 1826; owing to a series of delays and mishaps, however, the North American delegates were unable to attend.

The assumption underlying the original theory of hemispheric unity was that the newly independent American states were bound together by a common belief in the republican-democratic ideal. But a democratic institutional order failed to materialize in most of the Latin American countries. The United States witnessed first with moral indignation and later with selfish pragmatism how, under the screen of grandiloquent constitutions, corrupt dictators ruled its southern neighbors in brazen disregard of the democratic values to which they paid lip service.

Intervention by the United States against such abuses in the Caribbean failed to produce either economic stability or institutional democracy, however; rather it spread hatred of the colossus of the North not only in the country directly affected but in all Latin America.

By the end of the nineteenth century both North and South America had opened their doors to mass immigration from Europe. As millions of individuals seeking haven from political persecution or escape from misery and backwardness arrived in the New World, a new way of thinking emerged that viewed the spiritual unity of the hemisphere as a corollary of its being a haven for the oppressed. In the United States, Eugene Bolton became the best-known advocate of the unity of the two Americas. In Latin America, some prominent political writers like Víctor Raúl Haya de la Torre and Germán Arciniegas echoed his thoughts. But after World War II, the historical conditions that had generated emigration from Europe changed considerably. The western part of the continent rose from the ruins of the war like a phoenix from the ashes, more vigorous, richer, and more independent than ever before; the Communist eastern half closed the gates to emigration. On the other hand, Latin America entered a period of economic crisis and dictatorial regimes that have not yet ended. At present, many of the crisis-ridden countries in South America have changed from magnets for immigrants to catapults for political exiles. Thus the Bolton theory has lost its significance as a promoter of unity between the two Americas.

In World War II, after some hesitation, the Latin American republics followed the U.S. call for resistance against the Axis. Brazil and Mexico made token troop contributions to the North American war efforts; Latin America made raw materials and food available to the fighting American forces; and—except for Argentina and Chile —the friendly Latin American governments checked subversive Nazi-Fascist actions; by the end of the war even Argentina and Chile had severed diplomatic relations with Germany and Italy. Thus, Franklin Delano Roosevelt's Good Neighbor Policy bore fruit, and at least diplomatic unity was established in the Western Hemisphere.[15]

The institutional development of the inter-American system in the postwar period gave the illusion of a hemispheric coherence that no longer existed. The Latin American intelligentsia's growing awareness of their countries' backwardness generated revolutionary energies whose main target was the United States. The radical shifts to the left in Guatemala in 1954, in Cuba in 1959, in the Dominican Republic in 1965, and in Chile in 1970 were writings on the wall warning that Latin America's political and social dynamism was undermining the very foundations of the inter-American system. The United States was denounced, as we well know, for putting down the leftist revolutions in Guatemala in 1954 and in the Dominican Republic in 1965, for excluding Cuba from the Organization of American States in 1962, and for the military coup against Allende in Chile.[16]

---

[15] On the idea of a united Western Hemisphere, see Arthur P. Whitaker, *The Western Hemisphere Idea: Its Rise and Decline* (Ithaca, New York: Cornell University Press, 1954), and his *The United States and South America* (Cambridge: Harvard University Press, 1948); Edwin Lieuwen, *U.S. Policy in Latin America, A Short History* (New York: Praeger, 1965); Roger W. Fontaine, *Brazil and the United States* (Washington, D.C.: American Enterprise Institute, 1974); and J. Lloyd Mecham, *The United States and InterAmerican Security, 1889–1960* (Austin: University of Texas Press, 1963).

[16] On the Arbenz regime in Guatemala, see Robert J. Alexander, *Communism in Latin America* (New Brunswick, N.J.: Rutgers University Press, 1963), pp. 350-364, and Rollie Poppino, *International Communism in Latin America* (London: The Free Press of Glencoe, Collier-Macmillan, 1964), pp. 93-94.

On the Cuban revolution, see Boris Goldenberg, *The Cuban Revolution and Latin America* (London: George Allen & Unwin, 1965); Poppino, *International Communism*, pp. 173-190; Theodore Draper, *Castro's Revolution, Myths and Realities* (New York: Praeger, 1962), and his *Castroism, Theory and Practice* (New York: Praeger, 1965); Andrés Suárez, *Cuba: Castroism and Communism* (Cambridge: The M.I.T. Press); Paul D. Bethel, *Cuba y los Estados Unidos, habla un diplomático norteamericano* (Barcelona: Editorial Juventud, 1962);

It is beyond the scope of this study to discuss the validity of these charges. Suffice it to say that in each case the United States directed its action against a real or presumed threat of Communist take-over and therefore continued the policy of its military interventions in the Caribbean in the early 1900s. But the fact that some earlier American interventions were followed first by such tyrannies as Duvalier's in Haiti, Trujillo's in the Dominican Republic, Batista's in Cuba, Somoza's in Nicaragua, and, more recently, by Pinochet's in Chile seems to substantiate the leftist argument that the United States is to blame for all the ills of the area—poverty, backwardness, dictatorial regimes, and institutional instability.

Yet, U.S. policies in Latin America have on the whole been characterized by the pragmatism inherent in the policy of all great powers in history. Academic discussions about the immorality of spheres of influence can, of course, be held; but so far there has never been a great power that has not maintained spheres of influence in an effort to protect its own security. The Central European power zone of the Soviet Union is a case in point; its ideological disguise can mislead only the credulous. It is another matter that pronouncements like the Monroe and Brezhnev Doctrines, setting forth the existence of such spheres of influence, are among the instruments of imperialism and are therefore outdated diplomacy.

Because of the developments so briefly described above, it is hard to find issues on which full consensus can be worked out between the United States and its Latin American neighbors. There is growing in-

---

Earl E. T. Smith, *The Fourth Floor, An Account of the Castro Communist Revolution* (New York: Random House, 1962); R. Hart Philips, *The Cuban Dilemma* (New York: Ivan Obolensky, 1962); Leo Huberman and Paul M. Sweezy, *Socialism in Cuba* (New York: Monthly Review Press, 1969); Herbert Matthews, *The Cuban Theory* (George Brownmiller, 1961); René Dumont, *Cuba —est-il socialiste?* (Paris: Editions Seuil, 1970), and his *Cuba—Intento de crítica constructiva* (Barcelona: Editorial Nova Terra, 1965); K. S. Karol, *Les Guerilleros au pouvoir, l'itinéraire politique de la revolution cubaine* (Paris: Robert Laffont, 1970); and Maurice Halperin, *The Rise and Decline of Fidel Castro* (Berkeley and Los Angeles: University of California Press, 1972).

On the Dominican upheaval in 1965, see Dan Kurzman, *Revolt of the Damned* (New York: G. P. Putnam's Sons, 1965); Tad Szulc, *Dominican Diary* (New York: Delacorte Press, 1965); and Lyndon B. Johnson, *The Vantage Point, Perspectives of the Presidency 1963–1969* (New York: Holt, Rinehart & Winston, 1971).

On Allende's Chile, see Osvaldo Sunkel, "Change and Frustrations in Chile," in *Obstacles to Change in Latin America*, ed. Claudio Véliz (London: Oxford University Press, 1965); Leonard Gross, *The Last Best Hope: Eduardo Frei and Chilean Democracy* (New York: Random House, 1967); Francisco José Moreno, *Legitimacy and Stability in Latin America, A Study of Chilean Political Culture* (New York: University Press, 1969); and Dieter Nohlen, *Chile, Das Sozialistische Experiment* (Hamburg: Hoffmann and Campe Verlag, 1973).

tolerance of U.S. tutelage in practically all Latin American countries, regardless of their governmental system. Friction over U.S. trade policies and resentment at the support extended to some U.S.-based multinational enterprises have turned even military and business groups, hitherto partners of the United States, against North American presence in Latin America.

The failure of U.S. policies in the area, and particularly the dying-down of the hopes vested in the Alliance for Progress, marked the beginning of a new era in the South. Latin Americans have become more aware that they must rely on their own resources if they are not to become an economic colony and cultural dependency of the United States and of Western Europe.

The vacuum created by this split in hemispheric solidarity is an open invitation to extracontinental powers to fill the breach, and their expectations of success are not entirely without foundation. There is a tendency in some Latin American countries to consider the adoption of a Soviet-type government as the only remedy for poverty and backwardness. Some intellectual revolutionaries look to Chinese or other versions of Asian Communism, on the grounds that the autochthonous pre-Columbian civilizations maintained communal systems of agriculture and that the Conquest destroyed these by superimposing on them its inhuman early capitalism. Yet none of these ideological currents have proved potent enough so far to revolutionize the continent. It is not only U.S. policy that has failed in Latin America; Soviet- or Chinese-backed guerrilla movements have also run afoul of the resistance of culturally alien environments and the traditional apathy of the Latin American peasant.

That some Latin American countries have recently joined the movement of nonaligned states points up the fact that their quest for a new place in the diplomatic design follows various paths and obeys various stimuli. On the outcome of this maneuvering will depend whether or not North and South America will find a common ground for action and the legal instruments to carry out such action.

### The Monroe Doctrine

President Monroe's message to Congress on December 2, 1823, epitomized an idea that germinated in the minds of the founding fathers, took shape during the wars of independence of the Latin American nations, and evolved into the guiding principle of North American hemispheric policies throughout the recent past.[17] James Monroe intended the doctrine to be a barrier to an extension of existing European colonies and the penetration of autocratic European political systems in the Western Hemisphere. Thus, the doctrine had both strategic and ideological significance. Strategically, it was designed to keep a balance between the military power of the Americas and that of Europe by stabilizing the European overseas possessions at their 1823 level. Ideologically, it represented a commitment to protect the republican-democratic ideal against inroads on the part of royal absolutism.

The nascent Latin American republics welcomed the doctrine as an umbrella over their independence; they also desired to develop it into a multinational convention. Unfortunately, their hopes were frustrated in both senses. The U.S. government refrained from applying its protective clauses in a number of cases during the nineteenth century, either because it did not see its own interests seriously jeopardized or because it was not prepared to go to war against a powerful European state. The Monroe Doctrine has remained, as we shall see later, a unilateral instrument of U.S. policy, and has never acquired a multinational character.

According to the advocates of the doctrine, it prevented the "africanization" of Latin America—that is, its being sliced up into European colonies. Yet its application was largely restricted to Mexico and the Caribbean. The refusal of the United States to recognize Maximilian's monarchy in Mexico and its acceptance of Benito Juárez's revolutionary government in 1858 are among the most conspicuous and effective applications of the doctrine. In another significant development, the United States protested successfully against the reannexation of the Dominican Republic by Spain in 1865. After the Civil War, references to the Monroe Doctrine by the U.S. government began to multiply, but always in the context of the Caribbean and Central America. Thus, the South American republics had to hold European colonial aspirations at bay without the help of the United States and the application of the doctrine.

As the doctrine was broadened by a series of corollaries to meet

---

[17] On the Monroe Doctrine, see Dexter Perkins, *A History of the Monroe Doctrine*, 3rd ed. (Boston: Little, Brown & Co., 1963); Donald Marquand Dozer, ed., *The Monroe Doctrine, Its Modern Significance* (New York: Alfred A. Knopf, 1965); Simón Planas Suárez, *Les principes américains de politique internationale et la Doctrine Monroe* (Basel: Verlag für Recht und Gesellschaft A.G., 1960); Frank Donovan, *Mr. Monroe's Message, the Story of the Monroe Doctrine* (New York: Dodd, Mead & Co., 1963); Knud Krakau, *Die kubanische Revolution und die Monroe Doctrin* (Frankfurt am Main, Berlin: Alfred Metzner Verlag, 1968); and Campilo García Trelles, *Doctrina de Monroe y cooperación internacional* (Madrid: Editorial Mundo Latino, 1931).

new historical contingencies, it acquired connotations that were at variance with its original meaning; and these corollaries cause Latin Americans increasingly to regard it as an instrument of U.S. imperialism.[18]

The codification of the U.S. right to police the hemisphere—a result of the Theodore Roosevelt corollary in 1904—was the culmination of a drama of mutual disappointment with the lofty principles incorporated in the doctrine. The Latin Americans viewed this corollary as distortion of the noncolonization principle into a sort of license for the United States to intervene in the Latin American countries' internal affairs. On the other hand, North Americans took a dim view of the degeneration of the southern republics into corrupt dictatorships that paid even less attention to the democratic principles of the doctrine than had the original villains, the European monarchies. Public opinion in the United States widely supported intervention in the internal affairs of those Latin American republics that, because of their bankrupt regimes and chronic institutional instability, seemed easy prey for extracontinental imperialism. As one prominent Bolivian diplomat expressed it: "In the eyes of Anglo-Saxon Americans, the Monroe Doctrine justifies all the aggressive policies of the past. In the eyes of Latin Americans, it is the pretext for them."[19]

When, at the turn of the century, the United States emerged as a world power, its leaders openly gloated over their country's might. President Cleveland's Secretary of State, Richard Olney, wrote to the British foreign secretary in 1895 that "the United States is practically sovereign on this continent and its fiat is law upon the subjects to which it confines its interposition."[20]

The history of the Panama Canal was one of the glaring examples of unabashed application of the doctrine by the United States. When plans had been made to build a canal on the Panama Isthmus in the middle of the nineteenth century, the United States agreed with Great Britain, in the Clayton-Bulwer treaty of 1850, to share control of a future waterway between the two oceans. The treaty was concluded in an era when the Whig administration in England had little respect for

---

[18] The Polk corollary in 1845 extended the meaning of the doctrine to cover diplomatic intervention; the Grant corollary in 1861 stated that existing colonies could not be transferred from one European power to another; the Theodore Roosevelt corollary in 1904 codified the right of the United States to exercise international police authority in the Hemisphere; the Cabot Lodge corollary extended the meaning of the doctrine to cover any harbor or other place on the American continent whose "occupation for naval purposes might threaten the communications or safety of the United States."
[19] Raúl Díez de Medina, "A 'New Deal' in Pan-Americanism?", in *The Monroe Doctrine*, ed. D. M. Dozer, p. 128.
[20] Perkins, *History of the Monroe Doctrine*, p. 175.

the Monroe Doctrine,[21] but as the canal project progressed the U.S. government began to try to preempt exclusive control of it. It denounced the building of the canal by the Ferdinand de Lesseps Company of France as a violation of the doctrine, and when the company went bankrupt, the U.S. government promptly took over its assets. In 1902 the Clayton-Bulwer treaty was abrogated, and in November 1903 an operetta-like revolt declared the independence of the Republic of Panama from Colombia. The new republic was a tool of the United States, which made a treaty with it assuring North American sovereignty over the Canal Zone.[22]

By a paradox of history, one of the most important examples of implementation of the Monroe Doctrine was the case of Cuba, a country that sixty years later would subject that doctrine to its severest trial. The United States helped Cuba to become independent from Spain in 1895, but imposed conditions—in the Platt Amendment of 1901—on the government of the new republic that made U.S. intervention in Cuba's domestic affairs part and parcel of its constitution.[23]

It should be recalled here that the Monroe Doctrine became a stumbling block to U.S. membership in the League of Nations in 1919. A campaign led by the most influential members of the U.S. Senate assailed the Covenant of the League on the basis that its provisions violated the doctrine; and President Wilson, anxious to ensure U.S. membership in the new world organization, managed to persuade his wartime allies to accept an amendment to the covenant that said that "nothing in this Covenant shall be deemed to affect the validity of international engagements . . . or regional understandings like the Monroe Doctrine."[24]

President Wilson's efforts proved useless. Adversaries of the League of Nations in the Senate continued their opposition; fifteen reservations were adopted, precious time was lost, and after Wilson lost the election in November 1920 to Warren Harding, all hope for ratification of the Treaty of Versailles and the Covenant of the League of Nations vanished. It is pure guesswork now to speculate about what would have happened if the United States had been a member of the League of Nations in the 1930s when the Nazi threat began to loom large on the horizon, but there is no doubt that the absence of the United States

---

[21] Ibid., p. 96.
[22] Donovan, *Mr. Monroe's Message*, pp. 129-144.
[23] Concerning the Platt Amendment, see Lieuwen, *U.S. Policy in Latin America*, pp. 36-37, 62-63.
[24] Perkins, *History of the Monroe Doctrine*, p. 294.

prevented the League from serving as an effective instrument for maintaining peace.

The withdrawal of the United States from active participation in European affairs in 1919 would be the last instance in which the policy of hemispheric isolation prevailed for some time over North America's global commitment to liberty. From 1920 until the United States entered World War II, the hundred-year-old paradigm of isolationism was kept largely intact, but more subtle language was substituted for the outmoded terminology of the age of imperialism. In 1930 a memorandum by Secretary of State Reuben Clark dissociated the Monroe Doctrine from the Theodore Roosevelt corollary, and in 1934 the U.S. Senate ratified a resolution of the Seventh Pan-American Conference in Montevideo that codified the principle of nonintervention in relations among American states.[25]

During World War II the cooperation of Latin Americans in the struggle of the United States against Nazi Germany and Japan was so spontaneous that there was no need to invoke the doctrine. With the exception of Perón's Argentina, the Latin American governments largely agreed with the United States on the ideological and political legitimacy of the anti-Nazi struggle. But when the United States tried to rally its Latin American allies to the cause of anti-Communism, the response was less spontaneous and less generous. In an address to the nation delivered over radio and television, John Foster Dulles had said that "the intrusion of Soviet despotism into Guatemala was, of course, a direct challenge to our Monroe Doctrine, *the first and most fundamental of our foreign policies*" (emphasis added).[26] Both the phrase and its timing were significant; in 1954 the U.S. government still considered hemispheric security its prime concern, the pivot of its foreign policy. Twenty years after that statement by the then secretary of state, the benign-neglect approach of the Nixon administration to Latin America signified a reversal of U.S. foreign policy, a new sense of globalism—or perhaps a loss of direction or purpose.

The attitude of the United States during the Cuban missile crisis in 1962 stands out as the most forceful application of the Monroe Doctrine in its history. The challenge thrown down by the construction of Soviet missile launching sites in Cuba has no parallel; no such immediate and geographically close threat existed in 1823, when the doctrine was formulated. The possibility that the continental United States could be destroyed by an enemy ninety miles from its southern

---

[25] Mecham, *The United States and Inter-American Security*, p. 132.
[26] John Foster Dulles, "International Communism in Guatemala," in *The Monroe Doctrine*, ed. D. M. Dozer, p. 168.

coast was something that had never even been envisioned during the two world wars. Yet President Kennedy did not mention the doctrine by name, although in his televised address on October 22, 1962, he referred to Cuba as "an area well known to have a special and historical relationship to the United States and the nations of the Western Hemisphere."

This "special and historical relationship" has now become a household phrase in references to Latin America, and it is indeed a more fortunate—although much looser—interpretation of the ties between the United States and its southern neighbors than was the Monroe Doctrine with all its corollaries. The Monroe Doctrine had come to be identified, in the minds of the Latin Americans, with the most blatant examples of U.S. imperialism. The right granted by its corollaries to intervene in the internal affairs of the Latin American republics can no longer be exercised, since a continent-wide wave of protest and an embarrassing loss of face would undoubtedly result; and a return to its original meaning—hemispheric isolationism—is hardly feasible under the modern technology of communications.

Yet the claim of the United States to primacy in the Western Hemisphere and its rejection of the influence of other powers are justified. The only question is how to exercise this right without hurting the national pride of our southern neighbors and without tarnishing the image of the United States in the world. Declarations setting forth such claims are two-edged swords. Given the tense atmosphere prevailing in Latin America, any reference to the Monroe Doctrine might do more harm than good to the U.S. image in Latin America by immediately conjuring up the image of a viciously egoistic United States that arrogantly disregards the rights of its neighbors.

In sum, the Monroe Doctrine is at present a relic of history, and hemispheric leadership should be exercised by the United States through more subtle instruments of diplomacy.

# 3
# The Economic Conflict

*The United States seems destined by Providence to plague America with misery in the name of liberty.*

SIMÓN BOLÍVAR[1]

*Experience demonstrated conclusively that under appropriate conditions, industrial skills can be learned by any people, race, or human group, and that countries poorly endowed with natural resources can achieve high levels of per capita output and income.*

ALBERT O. HIRSCHMAN[2]

### The Historical Background

Eudocio Ravines observed that in Latin America Ortega y Gasset's unity between man and his environment is still missing: "Man finds at every instant that nature overwhelms him, makes him feel himself as a shipwrecked person in a sea of unknown forces."[3]

Man's dependence on the cosmic powers of nature often gives a melancholy touch to literature in Latin America. Earthquakes, storms, droughts, insurmountable mountain barriers, and impenetrable jungles are frequent settings for novels whose authors want to show that Latin Americans "move in a world out of proportion to human dimensions."[4]

The unchanging, torrid heat of the tropical areas, unlike the more stimulating winter-spring-summer-fall seasons of the temperate climates, undoubtedly makes a man less able to engage in the heavy daily routine of an industrial worker. The need to provide adequate heating in cold and temperate climates has always been a strong stimulus for productive labor.

---

[1] Quoted by Alonso Aguilar, *Pan-Americanism from Monroe to the Present—A View from the Other Side* (New York: Monthly Review Press, 1968), p. 1.
[2] *The Strategy of Economic Development* (New Haven: Yale University Press, 1958), p. 2.
[3] Ravines, *America Latina*, p. 21.
[4] Ibid., p. 21.

The rugged surface of the Latin American subcontinent, with its mountains, jungles, and winding rivers, has tended to isolate human communities from each other. The location of towns and villages in the midst of tropical forests in the Amazon, or in the sierras of the Andes, makes the transport of goods as difficult as the transmission of ideas. Although the radio and the airplane have surmounted many of these barriers, they have not solved the problem altogether. The magnitude of the problem can be illustrated by the fact that in the middle of the twentieth century independent Communist republics were able to survive for years in the remote valleys of conservative Colombia.

In many areas of Latin America—for instance, in northeastern Brazil or on the high plateau of Mexico—rains are irregular and droughts frequent. In others, like Uruguay and the Argentine pampa, where the climate is more benign, the top soil is sometimes so thin and so liable to erosion that extensive tilling is impracticable, thereby making livestock raising virtually the only profitable line of agriculture. Such natural conditions are unfavorable to the type of pioneer farming developed in North America.

The expanse of unoccupied lands was a challenge to the colonizers, who sought to carve out large areas for themselves with the help of native labor, thereby providing a basis for future latifundia. To the south of the Tropic of Capricorn, where indigenous population was sparse or resisted exploitation, colonization was delayed and followed trends similar to those in North America. In Argentina, the granting of vast domains as royal gifts laid the foundation for the latifundia from the very beginning of its colonization.

The province that was to become the Republic of Uruguay was distributed almost in toto to a handful of privileged individuals. Landed estates of over 200,000 hectares were given out as a matter of course. After the Jesuits were expelled in 1767, their extensive properties were passed on to lay landowners.

In C. H. Harings's opinion, "Of the various moral and material factors that contributed to create and maintain an aristocracy in the Spanish-American colonies—differences of race, economic legislation, religion, land tenure—the last was probably the most important and was the nucleus of most fortunes." And he goes on to say that "a minority of fortunate land-owning creoles lived much like their Spanish ancestors, imbued with similar aristocratic prejudices and with similar improvidence and lack of foresight."[5]

In the United States, the land tenure created by the colonial regime was swept away by the American Revolution, and the Homestead

---

[5] Haring, *Spanish Empire in America*, p. 241.

Act of 1862 helped to divide the cropland into sound, medium-size farming units. In Latin America, on the other hand, the system of primogeniture, according to which landed property was inherited by the eldest son or the nearest kinsman, kept the latifundia intact. Thus the wealth of the landowner class was preserved, and at the same time that the vast majority of the population was prevented from acquiring land, there was little if any land available for prospective settlers.

Even after independence was won, legislation most often favored the large landowners at the expense of the rural masses. When the Indian communal properties were abolished, the land passed from the Indians to rich landowners and capitalists, who bought it at incredibly low prices. This marked the beginning of the proletarization of the rural population; the new proletarians worked on the large estates as cheap farmhands. The abolition of the Church's mortmains initiated a similar process. These were bought up by the great landowners, increasing even more the already extensive system of haciendas.[6]

Thus, at the end of the 1920s the great landowner was still very much like his predecessor, the colonial *encomendero*. He not only possessed the land but also ruled over its occupants. Thanks to an inverted interpretation of his position, he did not attribute his power to the fact that he owned large tracts of land but believed his power was ancestrally inherited, and that this entitled him to own land.

The latifundium or hacienda (*fazenda*, as it is called in Brazil, or *estancia* in Argentina and Uruguay) remains the basic unit of agriculture in much of Latin America. It occupies the best croplands, and its cultivation is extensive and uneconomic. At the other end of the scale, the minifundia—small plots—represent the prevailing unit and are as uneconomic as the latifundia.[7]

Industrialization in Latin America faced the obstacles of poor energy reserves and huge transportation barriers. Coal, in small quantities, is available only in Brazil, Colombia, and Chile. The exploitation of hydroelectric power is still in the initial stages. Although Venezuelan oil is a rich source of energy and could be a powerful stimulus to industrial development, its domestic use is still limited because of low industrialization. Nuclear energy, which may one day become the answer to the hemisphere's energy shortage, is at present too expensive to allow broad utilization.

Independence did not bring about radical changes in the economic

---

[6] Fernán Torres León, *La estructura económico-social colombina en su proceso histórico*, unedited working paper (Bogotá, 1966), p. 37.

[7] See Frank Tannenbaum's chapter on "The Hacienda" in his *Ten Keys to Latin America* (New York: Alfred A. Knopf, 1962), pp. 77-94.

and social life of the new republics. The traditional rural sector with its declining living standards has perpetuated an ancestral way of life. Compounding low agricultural production is the fact that the handicraft products of the rural artisans have lost their value and marketability owing to the invasion of cheap imported and domestic manufactured products. Thus, with natural conditions not particularly favorable to the development of a modern industrial economy, and given the burden of rural masses stagnating in the backwaters of their colonial and precolonial heritage, two contradictory phenomena are apparent on the Latin American scene—sprawling cities buzzing with a modern rhythm of life, and villages and hamlets slumbering in ancestral apathy. The only contact between the two has resulted from the cities' need for manpower. Unfortunately, the large reserves of cheap manpower and the relative narrowness of the industrial sector have permitted the exploitation of rural labor forces according to the iron rules of supply and demand of early capitalism. The interplay of these two contrasting dimensions of Latin American life has contributed to the proliferation of shantytowns around the major cities.

### An End to the Vicious Circles of Underdevelopment?

The production methods and way of life of Latin America's inhabitants are still determined by the historical conditions described in the preceding section. They created economic and social structures that bear considerable similarity to the phenomena of underdevelopment in the Third World countries. In the last few decades, however, the economies of most Latin American states have shown developments that tend to break the vicious circles that paralyze the underdeveloped economies.

The first and foremost of the vicious circles of underdevelopment is the fact that population growth outstrips economic development. Latin America seems to have overcome this drawback. Since the Gross Domestic Product (GDP) of the area increased between 1961 and 1970 by 5.5 percent, and between 1971 and 1973 by 6.8 percent,[8] and since the population grew during the same periods by 2.9 percent, this leaves a margin of progress of 2.6 and 3.9 percent respectively. In other words, the 2.5 percent target set by the Alliance for Progress for per capita growth has been attained, and even considerably surpassed in recent times. Part of this significant growth, however, is due to the higher prices of certain raw materials, whose export weighs heavily in the economy of various Latin American states. As we shall see later, these price fluctuations produce great instability in the area's economy.

---

[8] *United Nations World Economic Survey, 1974*, pt. 1, p. 45.

## Table 1
### Average Annual Growth Rate of Gross Domestic Product at Constant Prices in Nineteen Latin American Countries

| Country | Period | Total (percent) | Per Capita (percent) |
|---|---|---|---|
| Argentina | 1960–1970 | 4.2 | 2.6 |
| | 1974[a] | 7.2 | 5.7 |
| Bolivia | 1960–1970 | 5.8 | 3.1 |
| | 1974 | 5.7 | 3.0 |
| Brazil | 1965–1969 | 6.9 | 3.9 |
| | 1974 | 9.6 | 6.5 |
| Chile | 1960–1970 | 4.4 | 2.0 |
| | 1974 | 5.0 | 3.2 |
| Colombia | 1960–1970 | 5.1 | 1.8 |
| | 1974 | 6.1 | 2.8 |
| Costa Rica | 1966–1970 | 5.0 | 1.9 |
| | 1974 | 4.1 | 1.2 |
| Dominican Republic | 1960–1970 | 4.6 | 1.6 |
| | 1974 | 8.9 | 5.3 |
| Ecuador | 1965–1970 | 5.5 | 2.0 |
| | 1974 | 9.2 | 5.7 |
| Guatemala | 1960–1970 | 5.6 | 2.5 |
| | 1974 | 4.7 | 1.7 |
| Haiti | 1961–1970 | 0.7 | −1.3 |
| | 1974 | 3.0 | 0.4 |
| Honduras | 1960–1970 | 5.1 | 1.7 |
| | 1974 | −0.5 | −4.0 |
| Jamaica | 1965–1970 | 4.3 | 3.0 |
| Mexico | 1960–1970 | 7.3 | 3.8 |
| | 1974 | 5.9 | 2.4 |
| Nicaragua | 1960–1970 | 7.4 | 3.7 |
| | 1974 | 7.7 | 4.3 |
| Panama | 1960–1970 | 7.8 | 4.6 |
| | 1974 | 4.0 | 1.2 |
| Paraguay | 1960–1970 | 4.6 | 1.4 |
| | 1974 | 8.0 | 5.0 |
| Peru | 1960–1970 | 4.8 | 1.7 |
| | 1974 | 6.6 | 3.5 |
| Uruguay | 1960–1970 | 1.2 | −0.1 |
| | 1974 | 1.9 | 0.7 |
| Venezuela | 1960–1970 | 5.7 | 2.2 |
| | 1974 | 5.1 | 2.1 |

[a] All 1974 figures are preliminary.
**Sources:** United Nations, *Statistical Yearbook, 1974*, pp. 634–636. United Nations, Economic Commission for Latin America, *Economic Survey of Latin America, 1974*, p. 178.

Table 1 shows that the economic growth of individual Latin American states was very uneven during the two aforementioned periods; certainly, the area-wide growth rates indicated in the previous paragraph reflect the spectacular economic development in Brazil, whose size and large resources influence to a great extent the regional total. No comprehensive data are yet available on how far the world economic recession in 1975 and 1976 and dictatorship and political instability in the southern cone of South America (Argentina, Chile, Uruguay, and Paraguay) have affected economic growth. As we can see in Table 1, countries with a very high rate of population growth have a constant uphill struggle to maintain a modicum of economic growth. Such countries are particularly vulnerable to world market developments and domestic political events. Just as there are considerable differences in the levels of economic, social, and cultural development between individual Latin American republics, there are also widely differing causes of stagnation or slow development. In Haiti the problem is still how to reach the take-off stage, while in Argentina and Uruguay highly civilized populations are handicapped by political instability. But even in these two neighboring countries, related by a dense pattern of human ties, the sequence of developments has been different. In Argentina protracted political instability may explain the economic stagnation, while in Uruguay economic recession preceded and largely motivated political turmoil. The fact that some Latin American republics fell back into stagnation after reaching relatively high stages of economic development is one of those enigmas that cannot easily be explained.

The second vicious circle that hinders the normal development of some Latin American economies is their dependence on the export of a single commodity or group of commodities, either agricultural crops or minerals, whose price fluctuations subject the exporting country's economy to strains that are difficult to counterbalance. The roots of this phenomenon can be traced back to colonial times, when the trend toward an extensive plantation economy and large cattle or sheep ranches predestined wide areas to monoculture—that is, the predominance of a single crop—that served as the main source of foreign exchange. The large reserves of copper in Chile and tin in Bolivia, coupled with cheap manpower, produced a similar emphasis on the exploitation and sale of these minerals on the world market.

Table 2 shows the disproportionately large share of certain agricultural crops and minerals in the exports of seven South American countries, and Table 3 illustrates the price fluctuations of these commodities within a relatively short period of time. The proverbial banana

## Table 2
### The Predominance of a Single Commodity or Group of Commodities in Selected South American Countries

|  | Percentage of Total Exports | |
|---|---|---|
| Argentina | 1970 | 1974[a] |
| Cereals | 28.7 | 35.9 |
| Meat, wool, hides, and other agricultural products | 56.7 | 41.8 |
|  | 85.4 | 77.7 |
| Bolivia | Average 1965–69 | 1974 |
| Tin | 57.9 | 36.9 |
| Crude oil | 9.6 | 25.9 |
|  | 67.5 | 62.8 |
| Brazil | Average 1964–67 | 1973 |
| Primary products | 82.0 | 66.1 |
| From this: coffee, | — | 19.7 |
| other agricultural products | — | 17.8 |
|  |  | 37.5 |
| Chile |  | 1974 |
| Copper | — | 77.0 |
| Colombia | Average 1966–70 | 1974[a] |
| Coffee | 61.9 | 47.1 |
| Ecuador | Average 1966–70 | 1974 |
| Petroleum | 0.1 | 64.7 |
| Bananas | 53.0 | 10.5 |
| Coffee and cocoa | 30.9 | 13.3 |
|  | 84.0 | 88.5 |
| Uruguay | Average 1969–70 | 1974[b] |
| Wool, yarns, and textiles | 35.3 | 7.9 |
| Meat and meat products | 34.6 | 25.4 |
|  | 69.9 | 33.3 |

[a] Preliminary estimates.
[b] Exports effected in January–August 1974.
**Source:** United Nations, Economic Commission for Latin America, *Economic Survey of Latin America, 1974.*

republics of Central America are not included in this table, nor are Mexico and Peru, which have more balanced export structures. Venezuela, with its foreign trade heavily dependent on the export of petroleum, has a special situation as a member of one of the world's

## Table 3
### Examples of Price Fluctuations of Basic Latin American Exports
(index 1970 = 100)

|  | 1971 | 1972 | 1973[a] | 1974[a] | 1975[d] |
|---|---|---|---|---|---|
| Sugar (free market) | 121.0 | 196.5 | 280.6 | 256.9[b] | 873.4 |
| Sugar (exports to the United States) | 105.6 | 112.4 | 138.7 | 589.7 | 431.8 |
| Bananas | 96.8 | 100.6 | 95.5 | 94.2[c] | 125.0[c] |
| Coffee (Manizales) | 87.4 | 100.5 | 126.6 | 136.2 | 133.3 |
| Coffee (Santos No. 4) | 82.1 | 93.4 | 130.4 | 117.4 | 131.0 |
| Beef | 120.3 | 134.2 | 178.2 | 184.8[c] | 210.0[c] |
| Wheat | 112.8 | 127.5 | 339.6 | 347.0 | 288.6 |
| Wool (Buenos Aires 5/6s) | 104.2 | 172.9 | 310.4 | 210.4[c] | 218.8[c] |
| Copper | 76.7 | 75.6 | 154.6 | 96.6 | 83.1 |
| Tin | 97.0 | 104.3 | 161.1 | 203.1 | 207.9 |

[a] Fourth quarter.
[b] In the third quarter the price of the sugar rose to 807.1.
[c] Estimates.
[d] First quarter, estimates.
**Source:** United Nations, Economic Commission for Latin America, *Economic Survey of Latin America, 1974,* p. 183.

strongest cartels, OPEC. The main point made by Tables 2 and 3 is that some of South America's key economies are still largely dependent on the constantly changing prices of raw materials on the world market. Table 2 also indicates trends toward more balanced and stable export structures. The most conspicuous of these are Brazil's thrust toward technological self-sufficiency and its export of manufactured products, Bolivia's and Ecuador's shifts to the export of oil, and Uruguay's change from a basically agriculture-oriented to a nontraditional pattern involving the export of processed agricultural products and chemical and other industrial commodities.[9]

Latin American reform governments sought a remedy for monoculture in land reforms that envisaged both a more equitable land distribution and agricultural diversification. A description of the failure of these reform projects would go far beyond the scope of this book, but let us recall that the most radical of these land reforms, instituted in revolutionary Cuba, also ended in failure, mainly as a result of overcentralization in agriculture. Around 1963 Cuba largely abandoned its agricultural diversification projects and nationalized most of the

---
[9] United Nations, Economic Commission for Latin America, *Economic Survey of Latin America, 1974,* p. 173, table 146, fn. b.

land. Beginning in 1964 the great socialist goal again became to achieve the largest possible surgar harvest.[10] The conditions of soil and climate on the island and the need for foreign exchange to finance industrialization drove the socialist government back to monoculture.

In other Latin American countries the failure of the rather half-hearted agrarian reform projects was less conspicuous but no less conclusive. It became evident that redistributing the land posed enormous difficulties, owing both to the resistance of the influential landowners and to the weakness of those on the receiving end. The transition from extensive cultivation to intensive small-scale farming requires above all a sturdy, hard-working, and knowledgeable peasant class, able to take over the task of the large landowners; and the Latin American peasants have not been historically conditioned to meet these requirements. On the other hand, since the end of World War II, landed property and farming methods have undergone fundamental changes. The ideal of the early 1950s—a small family farm just big enough to provide a reasonable livelihood for the peasant household—is largely a thing of the past in both the developed countries and the socialist world. While in the West the trend points to the growth of individual farms and the creation of voluntary cooperatives, in the socialist states a forced system of cooperative state farms has stamped out the ancestral peasant way of life.

Industrialization and the magnetism of city life have generated what some sociologists call the exodus from the villages. The migration of peasant masses to towns and the depopulation of the countryside are worldwide phenomena and, given the manpower needs of industry and the underemployment resulting from the mechanization of agriculture, they are a logical and even useful development. In Latin America, however, as in many developing countries, industry has proved incapable of absorbing the rural proletariat flooding into the cities, and mechanization is too limited to compensate for the manpower leaving the countryside. Owing to the introduction of highly automated manufacturing processes, industry cannot produce enough jobs. Thus, although the number of people employed in agriculture decreased from 53.4 percent of the population in 1950 to 42.2 percent in 1969, the bulk of those who abandoned agriculture did not become factory workers but swelled the sectors described as "miscellaneous services or unspecified activities," which now employ 22.9 percent of the labor force.[11]

---

[10] Dumont, *Cuba—est-il socialiste?*, p. 41.
[11] Quoted from U.N. sources in a report by Governor Nelson A. Rockefeller, *U.S. Presidential Mission for the Western Hemisphere: Rockefeller Report on the Americas* (Chicago: New York Times edition, 1969), p. 108.

Thus we find another vicious circle, this time involving the uprooted peasants who lapse back into the misery from which they tried to escape by migrating to the cities. In addition to its social aspect, this phenomenon has a moral and cultural dimension. Rural inhabitants swept into the urban melting pot may lose the virtues of family feeling, religion, and moral fiber imbued in them by their village background. At first glance, the abject poverty and crowded housing conditions of slum dwellers may suggest that they are the substratum of a new decadent, cynical, and anarchistic proletariat. But a closer look into their lives and mores leads to entirely different conclusions. A recent sociological study criticizes the derogatory attribute "marginal" appended to the inhabitants of the *favelas* (the hillside slums in Rio de Janeiro) as a middle-class invention intended to maliciously isolate this section of the proletariat from the rest of the working class, and used as a justification for the rule of the bourgeoisie. "Favelados are generally system-supportive and see the government not as evil but as doing its best to understand and help people like themselves. . . . *they have the aspirations of the bourgeoisie, the perseverance of pioneers, and the values of patriots.*"[12] Its author is not the only one to see the squatter movement as promoting national consciousness and enabling the backward rural masses to join the mainstream of the nation. This is particularly relevant in the Andean countries, where Indian peasants settling in the cities come for the first time into real contact with the Spanish cultural milieu of the nation. Their children go to schools or even universities, which enables them to be absorbed by the Hispanic cultural community on whose fringes they have lived for five hundred years.

The vicious circle of the inflationary process is one of the most contemporary and striking characteristics of the Latin American economy. The Keynesian concept of creating purchasing power by public spending, and a reckless proclivity to undertake foreign loans regardless of the state's capacity to repay them, are the basic ingredients of spiralling inflation in the area. Rising prices usually lead to labor disputes and strikes; inflationary periods hinder investment and slow down production, creating shortages of consumer goods, which in turn push up prices; the declining value of domestic currency drives up the prices

---

[12] Janice E. Perlman, *The Myth of Marginality, Urban Poverty and Politics in Rio de Janeiro* (Berkeley and Los Angeles: University of California Press, 1976), p. 243. See also Howard Handelman, "The Political Mobilization of Urban Squatter Elements," *Latin American Research Review*, vol. 10, no. 2 (Summer 1975), pp. 35-72, and Wayne A. Cornelius, "Urbanization and Political Demand-Making: Political Participation among the Migrant Poor in Latin American Cities," *The American Political Science Review*, vol. 68, no. 3 (September 1974), pp. 1125-1146.

of imported goods, and export profits soar—all these are factors in inflation.

As noted above, recently economic progress has outstripped the rate of population increase, but does this mean that the impoverished masses of Latin America now enjoy a better standard of living? Unfortunately, an in-depth analysis shows the contrary. In Brazil, for example, the per capita GDP has doubled since 1956, yet the share of the low-income categories, who make up 80 percent of the population, declined from 45.63 percent in 1960 to 37.76 percent in 1970, while that of the top 20 percent, in terms of income, rose from 27.69 to 34.86 percent. In other words, the standard of living of those in the low-income brackets increased by 1.6 percent annually, while the figure for the upper 20 percent of the population was 7.0.[13]

Osvaldo Sunkel suggests an analytical framework in which the capitalist system, viewed internationally, is divided into a dynamic, productive, and innovative center—which he calls the transnational core—and a stagnant periphery. As part of the international capitalist system, the dynamic transnational core overlaps the national economies in both developed and underdeveloped countries; but while in the former this core predominates, in the latter the reverse is true.[14] Of all the vicious circles mentioned here, the constant flow of wealth into the hands of the wealthiest is perhaps the most frustrating and difficult to counter.

The material conditions necessary for economic development must also take into consideration the development of human potentials. Industrialization requires skilled manpower with at least an elementary education and vocational training. In Japan, for example, literacy came first; industrialization and the unfolding of a capitalist system followed. As expanding industry called for skilled manpower, a large number of literate Japanese were available to fill the need. In Latin America the reverse happened. Attempts to industrialize have been and are still handicapped by a lack of skilled manpower and a well-trained technical and managerial staff. In Japan, intellectuals were ready to adopt western academic traditions, giving up at least some of their own ancestral and cultural patrimony.[15] Latin Americans proudly refuse to do this. They

---

[13] Manfred Nitsch, *Brasilien: Sozio-Ökonomische und Innenpolitische Aspekte des "Brasilianischen Entwicklungsmodells"* (Ebenhausen: Stiftung für Wissenschaft und Politik, 1975), p. 81.

[14] Osvaldo Sunkel, "External Economic Relationships and the Process of Development: Suggestions for an Alternative Analytical Framework," in *Latin American-U.S. Interactions*, ed. Robert B. Williamson, William P. Glade, Jr., Karl M. Schmitt (Washington, D.C.: American Enterprise Institute, 1974), p. 28.

[15] R. P. Dore, "Latin America and Japan Compared," in *Continuity and Change in Latin America*, ed. John J. Johnson (Stanford: Stanford University Press, 1964), p. 231.

consider their cultural patrimony as on a par with North American or Western European civilization. As far as the humanistic values—arts, philosophy, letters—are concerned, their claim is certainly valid. Yet as Latin Americans would themselves admit, the values of technical civilization were not of prime concern to either their Indian or their Iberian ancestors.

This brief discussion of the ills that affect Latin America's economic progress leaves open the question of how these shortcomings can be overcome. The prevailing theory in the West has been that a duplication of the capitalist world's growth experiences combined with a democratic political system and equal economic opportunity for all is the key to the development problems of all nations, regardless of their climate and geographic conditions and historical background. The Alliance for Progress represented application of this philosophy, which presumed that a more equitable system of land tenure and of taxation set in a democratic political framework would automatically result in more active participation by the masses in production and in fuller integration of populations into their national political systems.

This concept underwent its major test in Chile under the Christian Democratic government of Eduardo Frei. We now know that Frei's experiment was only partially successful, and he was unable to achieve his program during his six years in power (1964–1970). Legality and strict adherence to parliamentary rules hindered prompt introduction of socioeconomic structural changes. Moreover, the reforms caused bitterness among the bourgeoisie, slowed down production, and increased the outflow of capital. Although Chile made substantive socioeconomic progress under Frei, the candidate of the Christian Democratic Party in the 1970 elections, Radomiro Tomic, was unable to repeat Frei's 1964 electoral victory. Apparently many of the middle-class constituents who had voted for Frei six years earlier shifted to the conservative candidate Jorge Alessandri, ultimately making possible Allende's relative plurality (Allende, 36.3 percent; Alessandri, 34 percent; and Tomic, 27.8 percent).

Some form of economic planning is indispensable to rapid economic growth. In the new African and Asian countries, five- (or more) year economic plans have become routine. But in those regions the new rulers' approach to their countries' economic and social problems is more pragmatic. They had to start from scratch, artificially creating or expanding the modern bases of their countries' economies. In Latin America, however, 150 years of independence have deposited a thick sediment of tradition, prejudice, and rigid attitudes. Paternalistic democracies, which loath planning and take refuge in nineteenth-century legalistic concepts in order to justify their immobility, are the most pointed examples of this handicap.

In theory, a modern, development-oriented military rule has the leverage to carry out structural changes without adopting the rigid pattern of a totalitarian dictatorship. The Peruvian military junta that overthrew Fernando Belaúnde's constitutional government in 1968 pursued policies that were for some time considered as a model for the functioning of this theory. However, the experiment of the Peruvian generals seems only to have proved how hard it is to shoulder the twofold task of economic development and social reform simultaneously. After nine years in office the junta found itself, by 1976, in a blind alley, with the country's foreign-exchange reserves depleted, its foreign trade and balance of payments in deficit, and its currency devalued. The conservative wing of the Peruvian military establishment realized that a continuation of the reform process would inevitably lead to emasculation of the military's power and the emergence of new power centers in the leftist cadres established by the land reform law and in the trade unions of the nationalized industrial enterprises.

At the end of 1976, General Juan Velasco's successor at the helm of the junta, General Francisco Morales, started to move toward both the restoration of some form of capitalism and a modicum of democracy. The government returned the anchovy fishing fleet to private operators, Marxists were displaced from key positions in industry, and new legal limits were set to the workers' share in industrial enterprises. In February 1977 the junta issued a political plan calling for free elections and the right of political parties to function under a new constitution.[16]

Thus, the Peruvian military could not hold at bay the adverse capitalist reaction to radical social reforms and the ensuing boomerang effect upon the economy, which usually wipes out the advantages that the masses should in theory acquire by a more equitable income distribution. Since it was not ideologically oriented, the junta reacted by moving nearer to a more traditional economic system. It may eventually restore democracy, as has so often happened in the history of Latin American dictatorships.

The dashed hopes for balanced economic and social progress in the underdeveloped world have given rise to speculation about an unconventional set of goals for economic development. Rather than an attempt to duplicate the living standards of the developed countries, the more modest goal would be to create a "livable" future for the areas now

---

[16] See H. J. Maidenberg, *New York Times,* January 11, 1976; Juan de Onís, *International Herald Tribune,* December 27, 1976; and Reuter dispatch from Lima of February 6, 1977.

suffering from extreme poverty.[17] This school proposes a development model that involves a wider distribution of the benefits of growth, even if this means reducing the rate of growth. Advocates of this model suggest that the vast majority of the population in a poor area would reach a better standard of living if the alternative of slower growth with more equitable income distribution were chosen in place of faster growth with a skewed distribution.[18] Thus, if we take the Brazilian military regime to represent the extreme of "middle-level, rich, inegalitarian dependence, Communist China may constitute the other, that of decently poor, relatively egalitarian independence."[19]

The theories by American scholars about development models for environments that are culturally alien to them may be interesting mental exercises, but they have little relevance for the future of Latin America.

### The Economic Bondage of Latin America

The foregoing synthesis of Latin America's development problems is only justified in this book insofar as it sets the stage for a discussion of U.S.-Latin American economic relations and, more concretely, their three cycles of evolution—trade, investment, and foreign aid. Each section of this tripartite structure has created areas of friction, all of which are potentially explosive. A brief description of each is given below.

**U.S.-Latin American Trade.** The U.S. share of the Latin American market, which ranges from between 50 and 60 percent in Mexico, Panama, and the Dominican Republic to a mere 20 percent in Argentina and even less in Uruguay, ensures a nearly monopolistic situation for the North in the economy of the South. True, the U.S. share of Latin American foreign trade is declining; it made up 38.5 percent of the area's overall trade in 1960–1962, and dropped to 32.8 percent in 1970–1972.[20] This can be attributed to the strenuous efforts of some of the economically strongest Latin American republics, like Brazil,

---

[17] Robert L. Ayres, "Development Policy and the Possibility of a 'Livable' Future for Latin America," *American Political Science Review*, vol. 69, no. 2 (June 1975) pp. 507-525.
[18] Ibid., p. 515.
[19] Ibid., p. 517, fn.
[20] *The Americas in a Changing World*, a Report of the Commission on United States–Latin American Relations, with Preface by Sol M. Linowitz (New York: Quadrangle/New York Times Book Company, 1975), p. 16.

Venezuela, and Peru, to diversify their exports and imports.[21] Their situation is more favorable than that of the Soviet Union's minor partners in Comecon, whose foreign trade relies even more heavily on the U.S.S.R.—from 20 percent in the case of Romania to around 60 percent in the case of Bulgaria.[22]

One of the main characteristics of U.S.-Latin American trade, however, is that it is asymmetrical; while the United States accounts for roughly 33 percent of Latin America's foreign trade, U.S. exports to its southern neighbors constitute only 13 percent of total U.S. exports. Moreover, 52 percent of this total went to Mexico and Brazil, leaving only 6 percent for the rest of Latin America.[23]

The relationship between the Soviet Union and its Eastern European associates is much more balanced. Approximately 40 percent of Soviet foreign trade is with the Comecon countries.

At first glance it might seem irrelevant to compare U.S.-Latin American trade with the Comecon trade pattern, for the roles in the Comecon are reversed; it is the major economic and military power, the U.S.S.R., that exports mainly raw materials to its minor partners, while the latter provide the Soviet Union with finished goods. Thus, in Comecon the colonial exploitation paradigm seems to work in favor of the U.S.S.R.'s partners, while in U.S.-Latin American relations the major power is the exporter of finished products. But to infer from this that the U.S.S.R. is in an inferior economic position vis-à-vis the other Soviet bloc countries would be a mistake. Comecon is a closed economic and political system in which the Soviet Union dictates the prices. In 1975 the Kremlin imposed a new price structure on its partners which

---

[21] Between 1965 and 1975 the changes in these three countries' trade with the United States were as follows:

| Country | Year | U.S. Share of Exports (%) | Imports (%) |
|---|---|---|---|
| Brazil | 1965 | 33 | 34 |
|  | 1975 | 18 | 28 |
| Peru | 1965 | 31 | 41 |
|  | 1975 | 36 | 31 |
| Venezuela | 1965 | 34 | 57 |
|  | 1975 | 57 | 34 |

Despite certain fluctuations which run counter to the general trend, like the increased Venezuelan oil deliveries to the United States as a result of the oil crisis, the decrease in the U.S. share of the foreign trade of these countries was striking. *Britannica Books of the Year* (Chicago: Encyclopedia Britannica, Inc., 1966 and 1976).

[22] *Statistical Yearbook*, Secretariat of Mutual Aid of the Soviet Union (Moscow: Statistika, 1975), p. 323.

[23] Roger Hansen, "U.S.–Latin American Economic Relationships: Bilateral, Regional or Global?" in *Americas in a Changing World*, p. 214.

entailed a major increase in the price of raw materials and fuel and a disproportionate increase in the price of machinery and finished goods. Moreover, the Soviet Union exacts from its Eastern European partners substantial contributions to the exploitation of its oil and natural gas deposits, as well as to the building of pipelines, cellulose plants, and other capital investments.[24] The growing shortage of raw materials in the world will probably strengthen the Soviet position and also that of the raw material and energy-exporting countries vis-à-vis the United States.

The United States has no institutional ties that would make its *diktat* law in Latin America. It did have political leverage for as long as the Latin American oligarchy and military were its faithful allies, but the alliance between the United States and the capitalist and military establishment in Latin America has been badly shaken during the last fifteen years. Economic nationalism has become the strongest driving force in Latin America, as it has all over the world. Political pressure must now be exerted more subtly than before, but properly applied it can be just as effective as the brazen imposition of the Kremlin's will on Eastern Europe by the subservient Communist parties that rule that area.

The Latin American approach to the problem of trade with the United States is ambivalent. On the one hand, Latin Americans urge the United States to buy more; on the other, they fear the political consequences of a rigid trade pattern. In any case, however, the barriers set up by the United States against imports of commodities from Latin America (quotas on primary products and high customs tariffs on processed raw materials and manufactured goods) keep U.S.-Latin American trade within definite limits. Latin America's desire for international agreements stabilizing the prices of certain commodities have been fulfilled with respect only to coffee and sugar. A preferential hemispheric trade pattern similar to that prevailing in the British Commonwealth and between the European Economic Community (EEC) and the former African colonies, though desirable, is not expected to come about in the short run. Preferential tariffs for Latin American commodities could not be set up unilaterally by the United States; such a measure might entail pressure by U.S. manufacturers for reciprocal trade concessions in Latin America, and such preferences, if granted, would increase rather

---

[24] Harry Trend, "Comecon's 'Year(s) of the Raw Material Supplier,'" RAD Background Report/29, Radio Free Europe Research, February 24, 1975, and "The Orenburg Gas Project," RAD Background Report/165, RFER, December 2, 1975, and "The Economic Burden of Joint Investments for Comecon Members," RAD Background Report/128, RFER, June 4, 1976, and "More on Comecon Joint Investment," RAD Background Report/214, RFER, October 12, 1976.

than reduce Latin America's dependence on the United States as its main supplier of industrial goods.

**U.S. Investment in Latin America.** The second most important U.S.-Latin American economic tie is private U.S. investment in the area. In 1973 this amounted to $14.8 billion, an almost 100 percent increase in thirteen years. Yet the share of Latin America in the general spectrum of U.S. investment abroad decreased from 23 percent in 1960 to 14 percent in 1973. In other words, Latin America has been quite modestly involved in the formidable North American private economic expansion, which greatly increased U.S. investment in Europe and in Canada. The most conspicuous growth in U.S. investment occurred in Brazil, where it rose from $953 million in 1960 to $3.2 billion in 1973.[25] It should be borne in mind also that investment in petroleum accounted for an important sector of U.S. investments in Latin America, and it was concentrated primarily in Venezuela, where the government of President Carlos Andrés Pérez expropriated the assets of the foreign oil companies against a compensation of 1.1 billion dollars.

From a purely economic viewpoint, foreign private investment is certainly a sound approach to hemispheric development. It channels not only capital but also technical and managerial know-how to the host country, and it also alleviates unemployment and introduces new commodities into the latter's market. In a word, it spreads "Americanism," which may be sneered at by the leftists and pseudoaristocrats, but which is welcome to the consumer masses. It has, however, certain political implications which may make it an onerous burden on relations between the United States and the recipient country. Whenever the government of a Latin American republic has found it expedient to seize a U.S. company, the shadow of conflict has been cast over its relations with the United States. The viewpoint of the Latin Americans can hardly be reconciled with that of the United States in this area. In plain terms, the U.S. position is that the property rights of its citizens must be protected in a foreign country. Even if the Department of State shows some propensity toward accommodation, Congress usually exerts pressure to proceed firmly against the small brother who has disregarded his big brother's rights.

The history of U.S.-Latin American relations during the last forty years is studded with conflicts over the expropriation of North American property by reform and revolutionary governments. To mention only the most salient, in 1938 President Lázaro Cárdenas of Mexico seized

---

[25] U.S. Department of Commerce, Bureau of Census, *Statistical Abstract, 1975* July 1975, p. 801.

the country's oil fields owned by North American companies; in 1954 the Arbenz regime in Guatemala expropriated the holdings of the United Fruit Company; in the summer of 1960 Fidel Castro's revolutionary government in Cuba nationalized all U.S. properties, the most important of which were the sugar refineries; between 1964 and 1969 the Christian Democratic government of Eduardo Frei "chileanized" the U.S.-owned copper mines—that is, created jointly owned companies in which the Chilean partner held 51 percent of the shares; in 1968 the Peruvian military junta nationalized the U.S.-owned International Petroleum Company; in July 1971 the Allende regime, with the unanimous support of the parliament, nationalized all mines in foreign hands, and the socialist coalition which ruled Chile until September 1973 seized all U.S.-owned industries and banks; finally, as mentioned above, in August 1975 Venezuela's democratic government expropriated the foreign-owned petroleum companies, and Peru nationalized the iron deposits and refineries of a U.S.-owned mining company in July 1975.[26]

This catalog of nationalization and seizure provides an obvious explanation of why American investment rose more slowly in Latin America than in Europe and Canada. Each move of the economic nationalists was followed by crises of varying intensity and significance in U.S.-Latin American relations. The leftists often use a conflict with the United States over expropriation of North American property as a platform from which to rally public opinion in support of their radical policies. The battle cry of anti-imperialism today arouses the entire Latin American public, from the extreme Right to the extreme Left. The invoking of U.S. imperialism as a hazard to national interests may topple the balance of power at decisive moments in favor of forces that usher in regimes antithetical in all respects to established U.S. policies. In choosing between protecting the interests of its citizens, or maintaining its long-range interest in security and friendly relations with its neighbors, the U.S. government may be faced time and again with agonizing questions of priority.

As nationalism tends to become a common denominator for both rightist and leftist governments in Latin America, the hazard to U.S. private investment in the hemisphere and the concomitant danger of inter-American conflicts may grow. The trend toward economic planning, nationalization of basic industries, and unorthodox income distribution patterns that exists in almost all developing nations has taken on such proportions that it cannot be brushed aside as irrelevant.

---

[26] Some of these seizures were negotiated with the foreign owners of the companies involved, and the compensation paid was in some cases fair and satisfactory. In other cases it came to protracted disputes and lawsuits.

**U.S. Economic Aid.** The third U.S.-Latin American economic tie falls within the relatively new area of economic aid, a topic hotly debated both north and south of the Rio Grande. Moreover, the U.S. public has not universally supported foreign aid policies; in fact, certain sectors are known to be strongly against them. Yet the financial aid the United States has given its southern neighbors has consistently been far below what it has granted to Europe and other areas of the world.

A glance at the statistics will suffice to convince the reader that Latin America has been treated more as a stepchild than a prodigal son. Between 1945 and 1972, total U.S. foreign assistance amounted to $173.5 billion. Of this, only $13.8 billion, or approximately 8 percent, went to the Latin American republics, and this included the aid stipulated under the Alliance for Progress.[27] Moreover, the financial help extended to Europe under the aegis of the European Recovery Program (Marshall Plan), and the money granted to areas threatened by international Communism (Yugoslavia, Greece, Turkey, South Korea, Nationalist China, Vietnam, et cetera) were mainly in the form of outright gifts, not repayable loans. These were provided in a period when the revenues of the U.S. federal government reached their postwar low of $36.5 billion (1948).[28]

Those were the heroic years of U.S. magnanimity, when American money poured into the war-stricken European economy and bolstered the defenses of the free world. In one of the most conspicuous postwar developments, the West German economy staged a miraculous recovery, and the nation became, with U.S. help, the most powerful and prosperous member of the thriving European Economic Community. The $2.3 billion pumped into Yugoslavia helped that country to keep its independence from the U.S.S.R., and spurred it toward a more liberal model of socialism. Greece and Turkey, which together received 50 percent more than the entire Latin American area, were enabled to resist the pull of Soviet ideological and military gravity. But the largest slice of U.S. military and economic aid went to the Asian continent (almost $30 billion) to help the newly independent Asian governments to avert chaos and to steer away from a Soviet- or Chinese-type communism. The usefulness and effectiveness of U.S. postwar economic and military assistance must be seriously questioned, however, in light of the events in China and Southeast Asia. As a means of putting obstacles in the way of Communist aspirations for world conquest it proved to be ineffective. Moreover, the global pattern of defense against Communist

---
[27] *Britannica Book of the Year 1974*, p. 800.
[28] U.S. Department of Commerce, Bureau of Census, *Historical Statistics of the United States from Colonial Times to 1970*, September 1975, p. 1116.

expansion had a rift in it, in the backyard of the United States—its sister republics in the hemisphere. This was made clear during Vice President Nixon's trip to Latin America in 1959, and by the developments that followed Fidel Castro's takeover in Cuba, which culminated in the 1962 missile crisis. The change in U.S. policies toward Latin America, exemplified by the Alliance for Progress, was motivated by the shock of these dramatic developments rather than by awakening feelings of hemispheric solidarity. The Latin Americans were in the best position to realize this, and they resented Washington's delay in paying heed to their demands for economic assistance.

**The Dependency Theory.** The hypersensitivity of Latin Americans, which derives from their state of underdevelopment and is compounded by their awareness of descent from an old civilization, has found comfort in the theory that their problems are caused by their economic dependence on the United States. To infer from one single cause a complex pattern of effects is in all cases highly unrealistic. Yet it should be borne in mind that the Latin is basically deductive—in other words, he is inclined to deduce from a single premise a series of conclusions—unlike the Anglo-Saxon who prefers to operate inversely, to reach a conclusion by plodding through various premises. Moreover, nationalists find the dependency hypothesis particularly rewarding, for it offers an explanation of Latin America's lagging behind in the race for material values that does not hurt their national pride, while it lessens their feeling of inferiority vis-à-vis the developed world. As myths and realities usually coexist in a doctrine of national awareness, however, the theory of dependency is in many ways relevant. After World War II the redemptory role of import-substituting industrialization was widely accepted in Latin America. The theory was based on the assumption that once domestic industries were able to produce the imported goods that made the Latin American economy dependent on the developed world, the area would acquire greater independence and flexibility in regard to the sale of its own agricultural and mining products. Since until recently the general trend in the world economy implied a growing gap between the stagnating prices of raw materials and the increasing prices of manufacturers, the idea of industrialization seemed even more justified.

Yet industrialization also required the import of technology from Western—mainly U.S.—companies or from U.S.-based multinationals; and Latin American economists became increasingly aware that this process was introducing foreign economic influence on a hitherto unprecedented scale. To cite only two examples from 1970: in Argentina, more than half the sales of the fifty largest enterprises—mainly industrial ones—were carried out by foreign-controlled firms; in Chile, out of 100 large industrial enterprises sixty-one had foreign capital, and in twenty-eight of these the foreign investors had enough votes to control the enterprise.[29]

Since foreign-controlled or foreign-influenced enterprises enjoy certain benefits in terms of taxes and in regard to the transfer of royalties and dividends abroad, they have expanded and tended to outstrip the weaker and more vulnerable domestic industries. Thus, instead of making the individual Latin American countries more independent of the developed world, industrialization created subsidiary economies with all the social and cultural implications of colonial dependence.[30]

Interestingly enough, the authors who describe economic dependency quickly jump to conclusions in the cultural sphere which go far beyond the real relevance of the economic ties. Such authors reject the cultural model created by dependency as alien to the Latin American identity. They consider the Western, Latin, modern, Catholic, and democratic attributes of Latin American consciousness to be myths that have nothing to do with reality. In their opinion, the national cultures of Latin America are nothing but a synthesis of capitalist subcultures, and Latin America's links with the Western-Christian world have, from the very outset, disregarded the area's geographic, climatic, and ethnic characteristics. They believe that from the Iberian conquest to the subjugation of Latin America there runs a straight line of abuse of the area's natural and human resources and that this must be altogether eliminated.

The sociological and cultural implications of the dependency theory constitute an ideological challenge that the Western world, and particularly the United States, would be wrong to ignore.

**Military Dependence.** Writings on the dependence of the Latin American armed forces on U.S. military hardware, technology transfer, and training of military officers give an added dimension to the extensive literature about dependency and provide a powerful argument for those who rely on a single cause in analyzing Latin America's chronic economic and social ills. There is no room in this book for a discussion of the theoretical aspects of this body of doctrine. The following is merely a synthesis of the facts that constitute its frame of reference.

---

[29] Ricardo French-Davis, "Auslandsinvestitionen in Latein Amerika," in *Latein Amerika, Kontinent in der Krise*, ed. Wolf Grabendorff (Hamburg: Hoffmann und Campe, 1973), p. 247.
[30] Octavio Ianni, "Soziologie der Dependenzia," in *Latein Amerika*, ed. Grabendorff, pp. 379-399.

For the sake of precision let us make clear that provision by the United States of financial aid, technology, and professional training is not identical with U.S. support of military dictatorships. The armed forces of democratic governments have benefited from such aid as well as dictatorships. Yet when a country provides military aid to a foreign government, the lines of separation between purely commercial and professional ties on one hand and political bonds on the other cannot easily be drawn. In Latin America, the armed forces inherited from the nineteenth-century struggle for independence a praetorian tradition, an unusual lust for power. And although the current military dictatorships are a long way from the nineteenth-century *caudillo* regimes, they still claim to embody the right response to the anarchistic proclivity of the Latin American masses and to the inapplicable foreign theories of civilian politicians. In the nineteenth century it was the *caudillo* who emerged as the arbiter between bitterly hostile civilian factions, and as the self-appointed custodian of law and order. Since World War II, the military has arrogated to itself the role of shield against Communism, and has obtained the blessing of the United States for so doing.

Yet the strong ties between the United States and Latin American armed forces are relatively recent; they are a post-World War II development. European influence was predominant in shaping the first regular Latin American armies. German military missions helped to build up the Chilean army at the end of the nineteenth century, converting it into a model for its sister republics' armed forces. Chilean military officers cooperated in the organization of the Colombian, Salvadoran, Venezuelan, and Ecuadorian armed forces. German military missions laid the foundation of an Argentine regular army between 1900 and the outbreak of World War I. A French military mission undertook reorganization of the Peruvian army after the latter's defeat by the Chileans in 1883.

Between the two world wars, German, and subsequently French, military missions were at work in Peru; Bolivia invited French and German military officers almost indiscriminately; Brazil, although far ahead of the other Latin American countries in the professional training of its military officers, invited a French military mission in 1919.[31]

After World War II, the United States acquired a quasimonopoly over Latin American purchases of military hardware, technical assistance, and officer training. In almost all Latin American countries, U.S.

---

[31] See Klaus Kindenberg, "Militaer und Abhaengigkeit in Latein Amerika. Fremdbestimmte Faktoren seiner instititonellen Entwicklung, seines professionellen Rollenverstaendisses und seines politischen Verhaltens," in *Lateinamerika—Historische Realitaet und Dependencia-Theorien*, ed. Hans-Jurgen Puhle (Hamburg: Hoffmann und Campe) pp. 196-203.

military missions and Military Assistance Advisory Groups (MAAGs) have been established. Latin American officers have been trained in U.S. military schools and in the U.S. Army School of the Americas in the Panama Canal Zone. Between 1946 and 1970, Latin America received a total of $1.3 billion in military aid, and 54,270 military officers received training in American military schools.[32]

Yet with all the aid and training they have obtained from the U.S. military, the Latin American armed forces have never developed the ability to participate in an extracontinental armed conflict. Obviously this has not been the intention of U.S. strategic planning. Latin America lies far from the possible theaters of war in Europe, the Far East, and Southeast Asia. The NATO forces and the U.S. Pacific fleet shield the area against aggression on the part of Warsaw Pact forces. Thus, the general assumption since World War II has been that the Latin American military's task is to check internal Communist threat.[33]

It was this assumption that Latin American generals used as a rationale for persisting in their praetorian role, for overthrowing civilian governments and establishing their own rule. True, the military dictatorships that came to power in the 1960s and 1970s are governments manned by the nation's officer corps, and it can be said that the change in most countries was from rule by civilian to military elites, rather than from broadly based democratic government to tyranny. True also that some of these military regimes have demonstrated a sincere desire to promote the welfare of their nations and have proved to be less corrupt than some civilian governments. Yet the fact remains that these military regimes represent a retrogression from the stage of democratic development that many Latin American republics had reached before the military seized power.

That military dependence on the United States and the trampling under foot of democracy in Latin America are in any causal relationship to each other is difficult to prove, unless one accepts certain arguments of leftist propaganda as facts. Direct U.S. intervention is believed to have been instrumental in the overthrow of Jacobo Arbenz's leftist regime in Guatemala in 1954, and in the Chilean military coup in 1973 against Salvador Allende. Yet it is well known that gratitude is rare in politics. Governments that owe their seizure of power to the help of foreign states are not automatically converted into satellites of their benefactors

---

[32] Ibid., pp. 206-208.
[33] Edwin Lieuwen, *Arms and Politics in Latin America* (New York: Praeger, 1961), pp. 208-209. See also Lieuwen, "The Latin American Military," *Survey of the Alliance for Progress*, Compilation of Studies and Hearings of the Subcommittee on American Republics Affairs of the Committee on Foreign Relations, U.S. Senate, pp. 93-127, and Hearings on February 28, 1968, pp. 299-337.

unless the latter can exercise permanent control over their protectorates. The Latin American military dictatorships are not such servile instruments of U.S. policy.

Latin American military officers are a proud group of individuals with no penchant for subservience. Even those trained in U.S. military schools must often have frustrated their former tutors. In 1962 the then Defense Secretary Robert McNamara made the following statement: "Probably the greatest return of our military assistance investment comes from the training of selected officers and key specialists at our military schools and training centers in the United States and overseas. . . . It is beyond price to us to make friends of such men."[34] Many of these officers have probably remained friends of the United States. But some of the younger ones trained in U.S. military schools eventually became guerrilla leaders engaged in a bitter struggle against "capitalism and U.S. imperialism." The Peruvian military junta expropriated U.S. property, pursued a leftist political course, and in 1976 bought sophisticated Soviet weaponry, including fighter bombers and tanks. The Brazilian military regime, together with Argentina, El Salvador, Guatemala, and Uruguay, which are also controlled by the military, rejected U.S. military credits in the wake of State Department reports on the human rights situation in these countries. Moreover, Brazil insists on going ahead with the purchase from West Germany of machinery for the enriching and reprocessing of nuclear fuel, a transaction that is strongly resisted by the U.S. government since it implies the possibility of manufacturing nuclear explosives. Ecuador, a member of OPEC, has paid little attention to U.S. wishes for the pricing of oil.

President Carter said at Notre Dame University on May 22, 1977: "Being confident of our future, we are now free of that inordinate fear of Communism which once led us to embrace any dictator who joined us in our fear." The challenge thrown down to the dictators has hit its most sensitive targets, the Latin American military regimes, once the stalwarts of U.S. policy in the hemisphere. Thus, by implication this statement might herald a new era in the U.S.-Latin American relationship and an end to the military dependence of the Latin Americans on the United States.

## The Alliance for Progress

The basic ingredients of the Alliance appeared in a memorandum presented by President Juscelino Kubitschek in August 1958 to the Ameri-

---

[34] U.S. Congress, House, *Committee on Appropriations, Hearings*, vol. 1, March 16, 1962, p. 359.

can governments, which mapped out an "Operation Pan America" for the joint economic action of the twenty-one American republics. In this document, the Brazilian president skillfully twisted the U.S. main policy motivation—the defense of the West—to serve the basic aim of the Latin Americans—recognition by the United States of the problems of underdevelopment and the consideration of joint measures to bolster the subcontinent's sagging economy. Operation Pan America was discussed at various inter-American meetings until its final formulation by the Act of Bogotá, which established a special fund for social development. The phrase Alliance for Progress was coined by President Kennedy in his address to the ambassadors of the hemisphere on March 13, 1961. The charter of the Alliance for Progress was adopted by the special representatives of all OAS nations on August 17, 1961, at Punta del Este.[35] Both the charter and the Punta del Este Declaration contain a pledge by the United States to "provide a major part of the minimum of $20 billion, principally in public funds, which Latin America will require from all external sources over the next ten years in order to supplement its own efforts." They also state that "the United States intends to furnish development loans on a long-term basis, where appropriate running up to fifty years and in general at very low or zero rates of interest."

To trained Latin American economists it was clear from the very outset that the U.S. financial pledges to the Alliance were not of the scope and character of postwar U.S. financial aid to Europe and Asia. It was obvious also that of the $20 billion considered necessary to achieve the goals of the operation, only $10 billion would be provided by the United States; another billion was to come from Europe, Japan, and private U.S. investors—that is, from sources over which the United States had no direct control. Unlike the Marshall Plan, the Alliance for Progress stipulated that subsidies or loans could only be granted upon the presentation of specific projects. Thorough preparation of such blueprints, with the research involved, public bids for construction advertised, et cetera, necessarily entailed a substantial time lapse between application for a grant or loan and mobilization of the necessary resources. Eventually, after all aspects of an investment had been scrupulously investigated, and the Latin American partners had completed their work with their usual disregard of deadlines, the mechanism

---

[35] See William Manger, ed., *The Alliance for Progress—A Critical Appraisal* (Washington, D.C.: Public Affairs Press, 1963); John C. Dreier, ed., *The Alliance for Progress, Problems and Perspectives* (Baltimore: Johns Hopkins Press, 1962); and Lincoln Gordon, *A New Deal for Latin America, the Alliance for Progress* (Cambridge: Harvard University Press, 1963).

of the Alliance still had to thread its way through a maze of red tape, procrastination, and dispute, sometimes with staggering slowness.

The United States was reluctant to give free rein to its partners in administering the taxpayer's money, and for good reason. According to conservative estimates, between the end of World War II and 1951, $15 billion of Latin American capital went into foreign investments. The political and social aspects of the Alliance for Progress were not of a nature to dispel the concern of Latin American capitalists for the safety of their money. The threat of land and tax reforms foreshadowed an era in which large landowners and business tycoons would no longer be able to enjoy their privileges undisturbed. Precedents were available to show that U.S. public funds might end up in numbered, anonymous Swiss bank accounts as a result of the interplay between public and private interests in Latin America. U.S. mistrust acted as a deterrent, even in cases where the presumption of corruption was hardly justified.

The $1 billion annual contribution of the United States to the Alliance was maintained roughly through the Kennedy and Johnson administrations; it eventually declined under congressional pressure as expenditures for the Vietnam War mounted. The structure of this aid, however, belied expectations that it was going to be a help in rebuilding Latin America's infrastructure under liberal conditions.[36] By 1969 Alliance grants totaling $110 million and loans to the tune of $515 million equaled approximately the amount of U.S. aid to Latin America prior to the beginning of the Alliance operations. By 1969 voices clamoring that the Alliance was dead were heard everywhere in both Latin America and the United States.

Though a careful assessment of the economic achievements of this historic project has yet to be made, the magnitude of the operations substantiates the claims that they were far from a failure. AID reported in 1968 that total investments in Latin America came to $115 billion in the 1961–1967 period, of which Latin Americans contributed about 88 percent; 6.87 percent came from U.S. public funds, and 5.21 percent from U.S. private investors.[37] The failure of the operation to reach its prime economic target—an annual growth rate in national income of 2.5 percent per capita for each country—was owing, in Latin American opinion, to the fact that while the developed nations provided aid, they at the same time limited access to their markets. The United States

---

[36] As Senator Robert Kennedy observed, "Only 400 million of the one billion dollar U.S. contribution represented development loans on liberal terms, the balance consisted of surplus food shipments and business-like project loans from the Export-Import Bank." U.S. Congress, Senate, *Congressional Record*, May 10, 1966, p. 9705.

[37] *The Times of the Americas* (Miami), June 12, 1968.

practices tied aid, which promotes exports of its goods to the countries being aided and helps its balance of payments. Meanwhile, the recipient country has no freedom to buy goods wherever it can and under the best possible conditions. Loans, on the other hand, are to be repaid with the financial proceeds of exports, or, if exports are at a standstill, out of fresh loans. The underdeveloped country thus gets into a vicious circle in which loans, instead of being invested in productive ventures, are used as stopgaps to achieve a financial balance, while the paying of interest on debts and the repaying of loans make it increasingly difficult to maintain the country's financial solvency. All this sufficiently substantiates the outcry of the Latins for better trade conditions, more stable prices, and fewer barriers to exports. It also explains their feverish search for export outlets, no matter what the political implications of trade with totalitarian partners may be.

The Alliance for Progress unleashed energies that built roads, schools, and hospitals, trained students, and effected land and tax reforms. Despite all the bureaucratic procrastination, unnecessary waste, and shrewd countermaneuvers of both rightist and leftist nationalism, its achievements are landmarks in some of the most backward countries of Latin America. Where it failed utterly and ignominiously was in its political program. The ideological blueprint of the Alliance implied a revolutionary change in the ancestral land-tenure system, modernization of tax laws and tax collection, and, above all, reaffirmation of representative democracy all over the continent. Seventeen military *coups d' état* in the eight years of the Alliance's existence have dealt a fatal blow to its prime ideological commitment. Venezuela alone has pioneered a policy of cold-shouldering the dictatorships, without much success in proselytizing among its Latin American fellow nations.

A current retrospective assessment shows that as a political undertaking the Alliance for Progress was doomed to failure from the very outset. In Europe, reconstruction and the ensuing integration of the six Common Market countries succeeded under the leadership of a more or less homogeneous group of Christian Democratic politicians, geniuses in their own right. Their political, social, and economic policies did not differ on essential points. They were committed to representative democracy and to a progressive form of capitalism which assessed the social functions of property in terms of the modern teachings of the Catholic Church.

In Latin America the situation was entirely different. To the oligarchies and their paternalistic administrations, the new role the United States assumed overnight could not have been more shocking. In the past the United States had been their principal ally in defending their privileges; now it suddenly appeared on the scene with an emancipation proclamation for the poor, underprivileged masses. North American diplomacy, traditionally a supporter of dictatorships that represented stability and protected private U.S. investments, now demanded a profession of faith in representative democracy. Oligarchs and dictators alike understood that this was the price they would have to pay for the promised U.S. financial aid. They signed the Charter of Punta del Este as meekly as their predecessors had accepted the Spanish royal decrees emancipating the Indians. They did it very probably with the same mental reservations and with the same pledge—we obey but we do not comply—as had the *encomenderos*.

The oligarchs avenged their "betrayal" by the United States first by stepping up the flight of capital from Latin America,[38] and second by discovering that they were nationalists and lending support to anti-U.S. trends, extreme leftist propaganda not excepted. As Victor Alba pointed out, the "concubinage" of the extreme right with the extreme left is a historical fact in Latin America.[39] The Communist party has acted as an overt or undercover ally for a long series of dictatorships, from Perón to Batista and from Pérez Jiménez to Rojas Pinilla.

U.S. policy makers may have counted on the support of a progressive, urban middle stratum, flowing to the left-of-center political parties and through them to the goal of the Alliance for Progress. But as shown in previous chapters, significant numbers of the middle class in Latin America have upper-class aspirations, irrespective or whether they are productive members of the society or parasites longing for positions of political power. They bear little relation to the middle classes of Western Europe, whose progressive attitude brought about the bourgeois-liberal transformation of the Western European societies.

An additional observation may be made within this context. Little effort was made by Washington to support the Alliance for Progress with an adequate publicity campaign aimed at the strata of population from whom adherence to its principles was expected. The new hemispheric policy of the United States, in contrast to its previous role as protector of capitalists, oligarchs, and dictators, was insufficiently publicized. Constant emphasis was placed on the material tasks of the Alliance—which in themselves put great strains on its administration—with the result that the ideological-educational aspects of the undertaking were neglected. Despite the introduction of a revolutionary pro-

---

[38] A speech by Carlos Sanz de Santamaría to the Sixth Inter-American Conference of the Construction Industry in Bogotá, as reported by *The Times of the Americas*, September 25, 1968.

[39] Victor Alba, *Alliance without Allies—the Mythology of Progress in Latin America* (New York: Praeger, 1965), p. 147.

gram, the North American propaganda organs stuck to an orthodox propaganda platform and the disasters of Communism. Economists, sociologists, historians, and, last but not least, writers and poets did not seriously consider the impact of the socioeconomic transformation that the United States was mapping in the hemisphere. No in-depth analysis was made to find out how the new U.S. policy would reverberate in an environment alien and, to some extent, hostile to the new concepts. The administration of the Alliance was left, by and large, to bureaucrats who were unable to transform it into a socioeconomic doctrine of serious impact.

If we regard the oligarchy as basically hostile to the Alliance, and the democratic left as too inept to pick up the gauntlet, the technocratic military would seem to be the logical potential partner to direct the enterprise. From a purely socioeconomic viewpoint, Latin American officers trained in U.S. military schools as administrators of a U.S.-sponsored socioeconomic reform process may not have been a bad choice. But the Punta del Este doctrine combined economic progress with social justice and representative democracy, which the military was not qualified to achieve.

By 1964 the political credo of the Alliance for Progress went slowly down the political drain amidst military coups, stubbornly surviving dictatorships, and the maneuverings of paternalistic regimes. Its pathetic destiny seems to confirm the validity of Victor Alba's assessment, written in 1964: "To ask the bureaucrats to act like revolutionaries, the technicians to view things in political terms, the oligarchs to renounce their privileges, the reactionaries to accept the democratic revolution, is to ask for miracles that could come to pass only in a political dream world."[40] President Nixon put an end to this dream in a speech on October 31, 1969, in which he noted with a touch of melancholy: "For years we in the United States have pursued the illusion that we could remake continents. . . . But experience has taught us that economic and social development is not an achievement of one nation's foreign policy, but something deeply rooted in each nation's own traditions."[41] This candid recognition of the limits of power by the president of the wealthiest and most powerful nation of the world does not, however, diminish the grandeur of President Kennedy's original concept of large-scale hemispheric cooperation.

---

[40] Ibid., p. 130.
[41] President Richard M. Nixon's address before the Inter-American Press Association on October 31, 1969, Department of State Publication 8501, pp. 1-2.

# 4

# American Diplomacy in Latin America

*Americans are eminently prophets; they apply morals to public affairs; they are impatient and enthusiastic. Their judgments have highly speculative implications, which they often make explicit; they are men with principles, and fond of stating them.*

GEORGE SANTAYANA[1]

*What is needed today is a major architectural effort rather than an acrobatic foreign policy.*

ZBIGNIEW BRZEZINSKI[2]

### Personality and Role of the U.S. Envoy

There is hardly any profession about which so many misconceptions and fancies have been in circulation since time immemorial than diplomacy.[3] The nineteenth-century figure of the stovepipe-hatted, tight-lipped diplomat in pressed tailcoat and richly bemedalled, has given way to a new type of bureaucrat whose forecasts are based on computerized records of economic and social data. Yet the stereotyped myth has not been totally obliterated. The new twentieth-century-style diplomat is allegedly little more than a human cog within the giant administrative machinery that determines and controls his most minute actions, allowing hardly any leeway for the deployment or demonstration of his own talents. There is more than a grain of truth to the talk about the decay of diplomacy. When the invention of wireless tele-

---

[1] *Character and Opinion in the United States* (New York: Charles Scribner's Sons, 1920), cited in *Santayana on America*, ed. Richard Colton Lyon (New York: Harcourt, Brace & World, 1968), p. 59.

[2] "Recognizing the Crisis," *Foreign Policy* (Winter 1974–1975), p. 66.

[3] On methods of diplomacy, see Harold Nicholson, *The Evolution of Diplomacy* (New York: Collier Books, 1962). On the cultural alienation of the diplomat, see William J. Lederer and Eugene Burdick, *The Ugly American* (Greenwich, Connecticut: Fawcett Publications, 1961).

communication put the diplomat within easy reach of his boss, the minister of foreign affairs, his sphere of decision making was dramatically reduced.

Does this mean that diplomacy has lost its importance altogether? Is it, by and large, immaterial who sits in the walled-in U.S. embassies of Latin America? Does it mean that a U.S. diplomat successfully fulfills the requirements of his job if he simply becomes well acquainted with the social, economic, and political affairs of the country to which he is accredited and, in addition, is familiar with the administrative procedures that an overgrown Department of State imposes on its officials?

There are many indications of the falseness of such assumptions. A number of recent incidents involving overzealous, clumsy, or even arrogant U.S. diplomats on duty in the Western Hemisphere furnish clear evidence that the personality, character, and ability of a diplomat still influence international relations. What do such incidents tend to prove? Do they reveal the whole story of the difficulties confronting a U.S. ambassador in a Latin American country? Obviously, an incident dramatic enough to lead to the recall of an ambassador is only one fragment of the intrinsic psychological conflicts between that diplomat's frame of mind and his environment. Peace Corps workers called this culture shock. The violence of this shock results from the cultural gap between the home country and the country of accreditation. As we have tried to emphasize throughout this book, the Puritan-Protestant-democratic legacy of North America and the Iberian-Catholic-individualistic heritage of Latin America are separated from each other by a historical gulf that is difficult even for individuals to bridge. An ambassador's adaptation to his new environment is certainly facilitated by the fact that he is in the company of his own family and his own staff, which in U.S. embassies is generally extensive. The great number of U.S. citizens in the larger Latin American capitals imposes heavy social obligations on the ambassador and cushions him even more against the impact of cultural differences. The embassy personnel and the U.S. colony socialize for the most part only among themselves, and this inhibits the formation of close ties with the native population, whose habits and attitudes are often quite strange to the average North American.

European diplomatic corps move more easily in the diplomatic rounds, which are looked upon by many of their U.S. colleagues with aversion. Western Europeans, moreover, lack the Puritan inhibition against entertainment. Most of them are very well paid, on the assumption that they need not refrain from lavish entertainment when their duties so require. Soviet and Eastern European diplomats obviously occupy a rather special position in the microcosm of a diplomatic corps in a Latin American capital. Their embassies are shrouded in secrecy and their movements are closely controlled. They rarely form individual ties with native society as do the free nations' representatives. Yet their parties are renowned for the sophistication of their cuisine and the rich selections of wines and vodka—testimonies to the vigorous survival of Eastern European traditions of hospitality.

One might now ask what entertainment and personal relations have to do with modern diplomacy. To answer this question properly one should take a hard look at the tasks of an ambassador and his staff. Their job is clearly twofold: to gather precise information on the political, economic, and cultural life of the country and to transmit it to the home office; and to serve the interests of their homeland by protecting their fellow citizens abroad and by enhancing the prestige of the country they represent.

But why should human contacts of old-world flavor be necessary for the fulfillment of these tasks? And what sort of contact can or should an embassy maintain with the local population? North American journalism has been clamoring, in recent years, for a lively contact between U.S. ambassadors and the local populations. For anyone even superficially acquainted with the intricacies of a diplomatic career, this is absurd. The picture of an ambassador descending into shantytowns and visiting the underdog, like a modern Harun-Al-Rashid, is taken from the *Arabian Nights* and bears no relation to reality. There is no government on earth that would tolerate foreign ambassadors nosing about in the rats' nests of its capital city. And the smaller the country the harder it is for foreign diplomats to approach the lower strata of the population—not to mention the dictatorships, which exercise close surveillance over the diplomatic corps in their countries. How then can a diplomat accurately observe the political trends, economic strains, and underground social tensions in a land that is basically foreign and may be even alien to him?

First of all, the leading elites usually reflect all the preoccupations, stresses, and political ferments of the national body.[4] The term *elites*, however, should in no way be narrowly interpreted. The business community makes up part of it, as do the political, military, labor, scholarly, journalistic, artistic, and religious leaderships. Ideally, an ambassador should have contact with all of them. This obviously poses

---

[4] As Harold Nicholson put it: "In every democracy, in every cabinet or trade union, power at any given moment rests with three or four individuals only. Nobody but a resident ambassador can get to know these individuals intimately or be able to assess the increase or decrease of their influence" (Nicholson, *Evolution of Diplomacy*, p. 111).

a challenge to the diplomat and tests his ability to communicate. It presupposes vast erudition, refined manners, and a facility for conversation. Mastery of the native language and a knowledge of the country's problems help, but are not a panacea for all the difficulties a diplomat meets at his foreign post. A brilliant, multifaceted, highly cultured personality can more easily find his way to the mind and heart of a foreign community than can a pedantic bureaucrat, even if the latter speaks the native language and is a walking encyclopedia of information about the country to which he is accredited.

An ambassador highly qualified by culture, diplomatic skill, and self-restraint to carry on his job need not be an area-expert or a talented linguist. He can easily go from Sri Lanka to Ecuador, relying on his staff's expertise and on the work of skillful interpreters. Tradition-conscious and proud Latin American elites certainly find a U.S. ambassador who understands their thought processes, even if he does not speak their language, more congenial than another who lectures them on their faults in their native tongue.

It seems that senior career diplomats, who grow into ambassadorial positions through decades of preparation in both the Department of State and diplomatic posts abroad, have a marked advantage over outsiders insofar as administrative and legal training is concerned. Their long years of civil service teach them to be disciplined, discreet, and efficient. They know the rules of international protocol and are well aware of the security risks an ambassadorial post entails. At their earlier posts abroad they have made acquaintances and acquired friends whose help might be crucial in their accommodation with their new milieu in a foreign land.

Does this mean that a presidential appointee is a priori unfit to fill an important ambassadorial post? Not necessarily. There are shining examples of good diplomats who crossed the Rubicon from business or law practice to diplomacy without any previous preparation for their new jobs. It is a man's education, learning, and character that count, not his profession. The motivations of a self-made businessman are, however, quite different from those of a diplomat. A businessman's temperament is geared to quick achievement, while a diplomat cannot and should not reckon with short-term successes. The latter has a more complex commitment; rather than conclude a few concrete agreements, he must maintain and improve relations between his own country and those in which he serves. There is little tangible proof of success in such a mission. Whatever an ambassador gains in respect and popularity, it grows out of a host of imponderables, ranging from his manner in giving interviews to his choice of school for his children. Obviously, he cannot do much to change basic conditions that may cast a shadow on relations between the two countries, but he can mitigate their ill effects by the attractiveness of his personality. Conversely, he can hinder or even damage basically good relations by a clumsy, inappropriate, or arrogant attitude. A person who, when thwarted in his endeavors, does not hesitate to relate this bluntly to his environment is unfit for diplomacy and misrepresents his country. The changing pattern of U.S.-Latin American relations constitutes a great challenge to North American diplomacy. In countries that are trying to shrug off the reminders of semicolonial subservience and that hate paternalism, the U.S. agent's sensitivity to the pride and touchiness of the local leadership is a sine qua non of effective diplomacy.

Yet the image of the United States as a technico-business society that places heavy emphasis on material values has been reinforced by the bureaucrat-businessman diplomats who have so often represented Washington in the Latin American countries. The humanistic aspects of North American civilization—its passion for the arts and literature, its spirit of sacrifice in humanitarian enterprises, its keen interest in progress in all fields of science, and its broad support for all kinds of intellectual investigation—have not yet made their way sufficiently into the activities of U.S. representations abroad. These aspects can be publicized by the libraries, exhibitions, motion pictures, and lectures of the United States Information Agency. But in a cultural sphere like that of Latin America, where person-to-person contacts still play a greater role than documentation, the person of the ambassador, his general intellectual ability, hospitality, tactfulness, and ability to communicate with all types of people remain the clue to a more sympathetic image of the United States.

The metamorphosis of the Department of State from an almost provincial organization before World War II into a giant apparatus has made the selection and training of diplomats a very exacting task. Professional know-how and security requirements have understandably played a prime role in the selection of officials. In the interest of creating a more efficient diplomatic corps, it might be useful to do an in-depth study of the subtleties of culture, manners, self-discipline, and ability to relate to a foreign environment that a diplomat needs to enhance his effectiveness.

### The Inter-American System

The oldest regional organization in the world has survived its crises primarily as a result of the U.S. determination to maintain it as an instrument of American hemispheric policy.[5] But the focus of American foreign policy making has shifted considerably during the last fifty years from what a student of inter-American affairs described as follows:

> For many decades, U.S. relations with the other countries of the hemisphere accounted for most of this nation's international involvement. Of the 50 times the United States sent troops outside North America during the nineteenth century, for example, 43 instances were in Latin America and the Caribbean. More than half of U.S. foreign investment at the end of World War I was within this hemisphere. Sixty per cent of all U.S. diplomatic personnel stationed abroad in the 1920s were assigned in Latin America and the Caribbean. At the height of this country's "isolationism" in the 1920s, active U.S. involvement in the Americas continued uninterrupted.[6]

U.S. involvement in two world wars and its emergence as a world power after World War II relegated the Latin American area to the role of a pawn on the American diplomatic chessboard. The inter-American system was built into a rearguard post for the United States during the Cold War, but forfeited so much of its importance during the last decade that it has entered into the most critical stage of its history. To be or not to be is the question raised by many of the bureaucrats of the O.A.S. in Washington, D.C., as their organization appears to be tottering on the borderline between existence and limbo.

Yet the inter-American system is deeply rooted in American history. It was Simón Bolívar, the "Liberator," who first convened the representatives of all American republics at a congress in Panama in 1826, in order to discuss issues of common interest. Bolívar originally did not intend to invite the United States because of that government's consistent refusal to expand the Monroe Doctrine into a larger concept of Pan American cooperation. Although he later changed his mind, the U.S. delegates never reached the congress and the first inter-American organization remained without U.S. participation for sixty-three years. After the meeting in Panama only three inter-American congresses were held, in 1847, 1856, and 1864, all with limited attendance. None of the treaties adopted by these congresses was ratified by enough states to become effective.

---

[5] On the inter-American system, see J. Lloyd Mecham, *The United States and Inter-American Security* (Austin: University of Texas Press, 1963), and Inter-American Institute of International Legal Studies, *The Inter-American System, Its Development and Strengthening* (Dobbs Ferry, New York: Oceana Publications, 1966).

[6] Abraham F. Lowenthal, "The United States and Latin America: Ending the Hegemonic Presumption," *Foreign Affairs*, vol. 55, no. 1 (October 1976), p. 202.

The second period of inter-American development began in 1889, when eighteen American republics met at the First International Conference of American States in Washington, D.C., and resolved to establish the International Union of American Republics. The conference also founded the Commercial Bureau of the American Republics, which became the Pan American Union in 1890. This period, which lasted from 1890 to the early 1930s, was dominated by the Monroe Doctrine—in other words, big-stick and dollar diplomacy overrode the idea of Pan American cooperation.

The third stage, known as the Good Neighbor Policy, began with U.S. repudiation of the Theodore Roosevelt corollary to the Monroe Doctrine in 1930. Three years later the Seventh International Conference of American States in Montevideo adopted the Convention on the Rights and Duties of States which was ratified by the U.S. Senate and which stipulates in its Article 8 that "no state has the right to intervene in the internal or external affairs of another." This period included the unfolding of inter-American cooperation in World War II, based on a widely adopted anti-Nazi ideological stand.

The fourth, and so far the last, stage began in 1945, with the Inter-American Conference on Problems of War and Peace held in Mexico City. This gathering adopted a series of resolutions that subsequently gave birth to the 1947 Inter-American Treaty of Reciprocal Assistance in Rio de Janiero and led to the foundation of the Organization of American States (OAS) at the Ninth International Conference of American States held in Bogotá in 1948. Future historians may also include the period between 1945 and 1948 in the Arcadian stage of flourishing inter-American cooperation during World War II. The war had still cast its shadow when the Rio Treaty was being worked out. The emerging structure of peace seemed to be fragile and increasingly jeopardized by Soviet expansionism. The Cold War threatened to erupt into a third world conflagration, and the rising prices of raw materials still kept the Latin American economies running in high gear. The pressure for social change was relatively weak. Latin America appeared to be one of the few blessed, peaceful regions in a world left in shambles by the war.

Yet the birth of the OAS occurred under unexpectedly ominous circumstances. The prelude to this new inter-American organization was played by the mob in Bogotá, where the Ninth International Conference of American States took place. The murder of a popular liberal leader touched off a mass uprising. The mob assaulted Bogotá's governmental buildings and the headquarters of the Conservative Party. The riots, which destroyed Begotá's downtown area, posed a serious threat to the delegates of the ninth conference, and the mob ruled the city for two days. But few if any of the North American leaders understood the full significance of this writing on the wall.

True, the ninth inter-American conference brought a fresh approach in economic policy making. Article 4(e) of the OAS Charter sets out to promote by cooperative action the economic, social, and cultural development of the Americas. But resolving the serious economic and social problems of the Latin American countries proved to be a task beyond the capability of the inter-American system. True, the pressing need for economic cooperation on a continental scale had given birth to a series of inter-American agreements. The Inter-American Development Bank was established in 1959; the Inter-American Committee on the Alliance for Progress was set up in 1963; the General Treaty on Central American Integration established the Central American Common Market, and the Montevideo Treaty set up the Latin American Free Trade Area—both in 1960; and the Andean Common Market was founded by the Bogotá Treaty of May 1969.

The importance of these international instruments which ushered in the era of inter-American economic cooperation should not be underrated. Yet in the light of progress achieved in European integration, the inter-American system lags behind in terms of both economic and political integration. The supranational organs suggested by Latin American economists for the above-mentioned free trade areas have not yet been constituted. None of the inter-American bodies has a parliamentary body, as do the Council of Europe and the European Community. There is no inter-American court to deal with contentious issues that may arise after common markets have been established.

The supreme decision making body of the OAS, the Inter-American Conference, is scheduled to meet only every five years, and in fact its meetings have been even less frequent. The Meeting of Consultation of Ministers of Foreign Affairs can be convened upon request by any member of the Council of the OAS, which then decides by an *absolute* majority whether a meeting should be held. Although this body has met more frequently, its working pace bears no comparison with that of the Council of the European Community, whose members meet practically monthly. One of the most important recent meetings of American foreign ministers, which took place at Tlatelolco (Mexico City) in February 1974, was held outside the framework of the OAS, and thus represented a challenge to the traditional inter-American system.

The apparently most efficient body of the OAS is its Council, a permanent organ composed of one representative from each member state, with the rank of ambassador. The Council has its headquarters in Washington, D.C., and has the administrative apparatus of the Pan American Union at its disposal. It is the only OAS body able to work effectively in crisis situations. It is the Council that has acted promptly (thirteen times so far) to apply the Rio Treaty in settling disputes between American states and thus preventing armed conflict. Central America and the Caribbean were involved in all thirteen instances and only three of them involved the United States (as the party against which the complaint was directed).[7]

In other words, in Western Europe bold steps have been taken toward economic and political integration, but the oldest regional organization in history is hardly better than a kind of League of Nations peace-making institution. This reflects a need that no longer exists in Europe. Although the postwar history of Latin America registers only one armed conflict, that of the "soccer war" between El Salvador and Honduras in 1969, a potential threat of war has arisen on various occasions during the last thirty years and the peace-making machinery of the OAS has been far from idle.

Yet solemn statements about "the desire of the American peoples to live together in peace and . . . to provide for the betterment of all"[8] are still rhetorical and have no major consequences. Many of the resolutions of inter-American bodies have not been ratified by enough states to make them binding, and many others that were ratified remain unimplemented. The traditional laxity in putting the law into practice has been no less harmful on the international scene than in the domestic sphere.

**The Cuban Case in the OAS.** In the 1960s there was an issue that seemed to cement the cohesive forces of the system, when the OAS, under U.S. leadership, rose to the challenge of international Communism and its Latin American variety, the Castro regime in Cuba. Few suspected then that it would be this issue that would lead to a dangerous division between the United States and its Latin American partners and pose a threat to the very existence of the inter-American system.

The first OAS decision against Cuba was motivated by an attack on Panama in April 1959 by a small contingent of revolutionaries, most of whom were Cuban citizens who had sailed from a Cuban port. The invasion attempts continued during 1959 against Nicaragua, the Dominican Republic, and Haiti. The Rio Treaty was first applied against Cuba upon the request of the Peruvian and Colombian governments submitted at the Eighth Meeting of Consultation of the OAS, held in Punta del

---

[7] Inter-American Institute, *Inter-American System*, pp. 122-153.
[8] Ibid., p. 331. Quoted from the preamble of the OAS Charter.

Este, Uruguay, in January 1962. The decision of this meeting was to exclude the Cuban revolutionary government from participation in the inter-American system, and to order the partial suspension of trade with Cuba. Subsequently, during the missile crisis in October 1962, the Council of the OAS, acting provisionally as an organ of consultation, called for the immediate dismantling and withdrawal from Cuba of all missiles and other weapons with any offensive capability. The Council also recommended that the member states, in accordance with Articles 6 and 8 of the Rio Treaty, take all measures, individually and collectively and including the use of armed force, which they might deem necessary to ensure that the government of Cuba not continue to receive from the Sino-Soviet powers material and related supplies that might threaten the peace and security of the continent.

Finally, in 1964 the Ninth Meeting of Consultation of Ministers of Foreign Affairs ordered the American states to sever diplomatic and consular relations with Cuba, and to suspend all trade and sea transportation between it and their own countries except for reasons of a humanitarian nature.[9]

Cuba's ostracism has never been complete. Mexico refused to subscribe to the OAS decision, and it continued to maintain diplomatic relations and air transportation with Cuba. Chile reestablished diplomatic relations with Cuba on November 12, 1970, less than ten days after Salvador Allende's inauguration as president of the republic. Although the military junta in Chile has since severed relations with Havana, the issue of relations with America's only Communist regime continues to be a hot potato at all inter-American meetings.

In April 1972 Peru's military junta advocated Cuba's readmission to the inter-American system at the General Assembly of the OAS in Washington. In June of that year, at a meeting of the Permanent Council of the OAS, Peru moved that diplomatic and other sanctions against Cuba be lifted and was supported by seven Latin American delegations—Chile, Mexico, Ecuador, Jamaica, Panama, Peru, and Trinidad and Tobago. Three others—Venezuela, Barbados, and Argentina—abstained, while the rest of the delegates voted with the United States to continue the boycott. A year later, in April 1973, the

---

[9] The government of Venezuela requested the OAS Council on November 29, 1963, to "consider the measures that should be taken to deal with the acts of intervention and aggression on the part of the Government of Cuba that affect the territorial integrity and the sovereignty of Venezuela, as well as the operation of its democratic institutions." The Council appointed a committee to investigate the changes made by the government of Venezuela, and the Ninth Meeting of Consultation of Ministers of Foreign Affairs, held in Washington, D.C., July 21–26, 1964, resolved to apply sanctions against Cuba.

General Assembly of the OAS adopted a resolution that admitted a "plurality of ideologies"—obviously a concession to the socialist government which then ruled Chile, but also giving leeway to readmission of Cuba into the community.

By 1973-1974 the many loopholes in Cuba's ostracism from its southern neighbors clearly showed that the United States was losing its grip over Latin America. In 1973 Peru, Argentina, and Venezuela re-established diplomatic relations with Cuba, and the former British colonies ignored the ban when they joined the inter-American system.

In February 1974, at the meeting of American foreign ministers (outside the regular framework of the OAS) in Mexico City, the question of Cuba's readmission into the organization was raised by the Colombian delegate and was immediately supported by Venezuela, Peru, and Jamaica. Only Brazil, Chile, and other rightist dictatorships offered the United States effective support on the question. Thereupon, Kissinger avoided a discussion on the issue, making reference to its resolution in a wider context.

**The Need for Structural Reform in the Inter-American System.** What may have lain behind Kissinger's reference to a "wider context" that would allow Cuba's reintegration in the inter-American system has never been spelled out. Yet, as the process of redefining Latin America's identity gingerly creeps ahead, the concept of a Latin American regional organization in which the United States would not participate gains support. It was recognition of the need for such a body that led to the establishment of the Special Committee on Consultation and Negotiation, which is an organ of the Inter-American Economic and Social Council (IA-ECOSOC) and of the Special Coordinating Commission for Latin America in the United Nations. Both agencies have served to coordinate Latin American positions vis-à-vis the United States and the industrialized world in general, and both have been recognized by the U.S. government as policy making bodies.[10] In 1975, Presidents Carlos Andrés Pérez of Venezuela and Luis Echeverría of Mexico proposed the creation of a Latin American economic system to be known as SELA. Its task and scope of action had been worked out at several meetings at which only representatives of Latin American governments took part. Although the original idea encompassed progress toward a Latin American common market along the lines of the EEC and Comecon,

---

[10] *U.S. Foreign Policy for the 1970s—The Emerging Structure of Peace*, a report to the Congress by Richard Nixon, President of the United States, February 9, 1972, p. 93.

the consensus reached on the sphere of activities of the new organization is more modest in scope. It embraces the protection of Latin American raw material prices against fluctuations on the world market and the promotion of industrial and agricultural development in the area; it proposes the phasing out of imports of capital and technology from outside the region; and it provides a platform for consultation among existing organizations.[11] The area of action thus defined largely overlaps that covered by Chapters VI (Economic Standards) and VII (Social Standards) of the OAS Charter.

Thus, there is a definite trend in Latin America toward the creation of consultative bodies which exclude the United States from membership and whose task is to promote the economic and social goals outlined in the OAS Charter. The main purpose of the new agencies is to protect Latin America against the economic imperialism of the developed world, and particularly from interference by multinationals in Latin American domestic affairs.

Can Latin America's struggle for economic emancipation from the United States be channeled through conventional OAS bodies, or must it bypass the inter-American system? The answer, obviously, is that the second alternative is the more likely. Another question is whether there would be any chance to establish twin structures for the OAS: one in which the Latin American states alone would participate, and the other a sort of coordinating agency for the United States and Latin America. Such a structure would respect the bipolarity of the hemisphere without excluding the United States from decision making on issues of bilateral interest. The Latin American wing of the new structure would be competent to deal with intra-Latin American economic and social issues (Chapters VI and VII of the OAS Charter), the pacific settlement of disputes between Latin American states (Chapter IV), and cultural standards (Chapter VIII). A coordinating commission with headquarters in Washington would deal with issues that involve the United States. It goes without saying that the Latin American wing of the OAS would have its headquarters in a Latin American country.

The OAS has a legacy of almost a century of U.S. tutelage. Its organs are bureaucratic and its procedures clumsy. It has lost the cohesion that a sense of common danger during World War II and the subsequent Cold War injected into it. In April 1973 William D. Rogers, who later became Assistant Secretary of State for Latin American Affairs, proposed in an article in the *Washington Post* that the United States should pull out of the OAS, which had become increasingly a

---

[11] Radio Free Europe Special Report/Volsky (Miami: March 25, 1975). See also Reuter dispatch from Panama City of August 3, 1975.

Latin American organization in a hemisphere widely split between the United States and Latin America. He also wrote:

> Formal U.S. withdrawal to some associated role would strengthen the organization. It would permit the OAS to concentrate on legitimate regional issues—the common interest of the nations of Latin America. It would end the accusation of U.S. domination of the organization. It would allow the U.S. to have the same observer status in the organization as the Europeans. It would say something to the Soviets about East Europe. And it would permit us to give up our painful and often ludicrous efforts to maintain a "low profile" in the OAS for the huge United States, an effort which reminds one of nothing so much as an awkward and embarrassed hippopotamus.[12]

Although in many respects I share Rogers's views, I would not go so far as to recommend a U.S. withdrawal from the OAS. For reasons explained in the previous chapters of this book, I believe that there *is* a special relationship between the United States and its southern neighbors, and the OAS should reflect both the unity and the diversity in the Western Hemisphere. True, the meetings of the OAS have recently become a sounding board for Latin American discontent with U.S. policy. True, Latin Americans usually arrive at these meetings with a consensus worked out a priori in order to face the United States with concerted demands. These have revolved around three key topics: U.S. restrictions on trade, the harmful role of the multinationals, and the question of Cuba's membership. On the first two issues the Latin American speeches have been time-consuming exercises in rhetoric, and the United States would save time and escape embarrassment if it could skip these rallies and be faced only with a resolution worked out by the entire Latin American community and presented to a more nonpolitical meeting of experts in the coordinating commission of the OAS.

The twin structures in the OAS would maintain U.S. presence in the hemisphere. The Latin American wing could gradually take over the tasks, defined in Chapter IV of the OAS Charter and set forth in a more elaborate manner by the Pact of Bogotá (1948), with regard to settling disputes by pacific means. This would leave the United States untouched by the petty disputes that time and again disturb the peace of the continent and might degenerate into an armed conflict like the

---

[12] *Washington Post*, April 8, 1973. See also Sol Linowitz's comments on it in *Washington Post* of April 11, and William D. Rogers's answer in the same newspaper on April 22.

1969 "soccer war." The new organizational setup would also facilitate the reincorporation of Cuba into the inter-American system, by making it a member of the Latin American OAS body. This would avoid the necessity of having Havana and Washington sit face-to-face as adversaries in a regional body, at least until their conflict has been ironed out.

A revision of the OAS Charter would include a review of some of the inter-American documents that form integral parts of the system, such as the American Declaration on the Rights and Duties of Man (Bogotá, 1948), the conventions on diplomatic asylum (Montevideo, 1933, and Caracas, 1954), the statute of the Inter-American Commission on Human Rights (1960), and the Declaration of Santiago, Chile, on Representative Democracy (1959). These documents provide an almost complete catalog of human rights. They provide for the protection of the individual against the tyranny of the state, and they stipulate freedom of opinion and assembly, the rule of social justice and security, and the right to due process of law. In view of the constant flouting of elementary human rights by the ruling dictatorships in Latin America, these stipulations are little but a farce, a true reflection of the Iberian tradition of noncompliance with the written law which is at odds with reality. Since dictatorships always have the impudence to state that they respect human rights, the Commission on the Reform of the OAS Charter has so far met with only one difficulty—the definition of representative democracy in the Declaration of Santiago. The dispute inside and outside the commission over the substitution of the term *pluralism* for *representative democracy* has reportedly delayed the work of the commission.

Reform of the OAS structure should of course not disregard the basic security of the Americas. Thus it should not affect the key provisions of the Inter-American Treaty of Reciprocal Assistance (Rio de Janeiro, 1947). While compliance with those provisions that refer to conflicts between Latin American states could be entrusted to the Latin American body of the OAS, the stipulations of Article 3 of the treaty should be a matter of common U.S.-Latin American concern. For this article sets forth that an extrahemispheric attack on any American state should be considered an attack on all, and all should assist the victim of such aggression to defend itself. The provisions of the Rio Treaty, if they are ever amended, should be brought up-to-date to meet the challenge of a nuclear war, rather than be watered down.

It is obvious that such an important change in the structure of the OAS can be brought about only by long years of courage and constant effort on the part of all involved. There is no doubt also that the United States would play a crucial role in the tedious negotiations that might lead to structural reform. But as J. F. Kennedy said, "If we are to meet a problem so staggering in its dimension, our approach must itself be bold."[13]

## The Options of U.S. Policy Making

As a first task, we should define Latin America's place in global U.S. policy. Theoretically, there are various options open to U.S. policy making in Latin America. According to one student of inter-American relations, the alternatives boil down to the policy of special relationship, the policy of pure globalism, and the policy of globalism with a tilt toward Latin America.[14] One might say that it is the latter option that has been carried out by the Nixon and Ford administrations, and it has acquired the rather degrading connotation of benign neglect. Both pure globalism and benign neglect are based, in this author's view, on a blatant disregard of the historical and geographic conditions of the Western Hemisphere. North and South Americans live on the same continent and are linked by a complex historical legacy of affinity and rivalry, cooperation and conflict. Their relations have gone through a number of stages—Manifest Destiny, the Monroe Doctrine, the Good Neighbor Policy, and the Alliance for Progress. After the failure of the Alliance, the links between the two halves of the hemisphere seemed to slacken. The frustration provoked by this misfortune strengthened the nationalism of the Latin Americans and weakened the interest of the North Americans in the South. Yet neither resentment nor indifference can change the fact that the two halves of the Western Hemisphere are basically interdependent.

Latin America needs the United States as a market for its exports and as a source of goods and technology. This economic interdependence, which undeniably has some colonial features, has created a potentially explosive situation in Latin America. It is impossible to overlook the fact that in the back yard of the United States there is an area with an excessive population growth, a lopsided economic and social structure, hotbeds of extremism (in the universities and some trade unions), and an extensive network of leftist guerrilla groups. It is an area that might become the spearhead of a radicalized Third World if its desperate striving for rank and identity should drive it into the nonaligned camp. It is also, however, an area that has a historical relationship with the United States. As J. F. Kennedy said:

---
[13] Gerald Gardner, ed., *The Quotable Mr. Kennedy* (New York: Eagle Books Edition, Popular Library, 1963), p. 60.
[14] Hansen, "U.S.–Latin American Relationships," pp. 231-238.

This world of ours is not merely an accident of geography. Our continents are bound together by a common history—the endless exploration of new frontiers. Our nations are the product of a common struggle—the revolt from colonial rule. And our people share a common heritage—the quest for dignity and the freedom of man.[15]

Secretary of State Henry A. Kissinger seemed to agree with this concept when he said in Venezuela on February 17, 1976: "The United States continues in this era to feel a *special concern* [emphasis added] for its hemispheric relations. . . . We feel strongly that our cooperation as equals in this hemisphere can be a model for cooperation in the world arena."[16]

Yet the presidential election campaign of 1976 was singularly devoid of pronouncements on Latin America. With the exception of the Panama Canal—on which, by the way, Ford and Carter seemed largely to agree—policy toward Latin America was not an issue. President Jimmy Carter in his first pronouncement on Latin America, on April 14, 1977, provided an explanation for this significant silence. He told the OAS Permanent Council that "a single United States policy toward Latin America and the Caribbean makes little sense. . . . Your economic problems are also global in character and cannot be dealt with solely on regional terms." Further on, the president gave another hint that the United States henceforth intended to deal with Latin American issues in the framework of the North-South dialog when he appealed to his Latin American partners "to contribute your constructive leadership and help guide us in this North-South dialogue."[17]

Is this a consequence of the global foreign policy that led to U.S. military intervention in Southeast Asia, involved the secretary of state in peace-keeping missions in the Middle East and Africa, and inflated U.S. commitments to global dimensions while leaving a vital area like Latin America outside the perimeters of immediate U.S. concern? Or did the failure of the Alliance for Progress deal such an irreparable blow to the hopes of fruitful cooperation with our southern neighbors that the reservoirs of good will toward Latin America became exhausted? And finally, is U.S. policy making so dependent on the lobbies of the ethnic minorities, Jews, Eastern Europeans, and others that it is forced to concentrate on areas that normally would not be of immediate con-

---

[15] Gardner, *Quotable Mr. Kennedy*, p. 61.
[16] Secretary of State Henry A. Kissinger's address at the U.S. Venezuelan Symposium at Macuto, February 17, 1976, Department of State publication no. 8848.
[17] President Jimmy Carter's address before the Permanent Council of the Organization of American States on April 14, 1977.

cern to the policy makers? This is in no way meant to diminish the importance of Israel and Eastern Europe on the global diplomatic chessboard; rather, it is to affirm the primordial importance that Latin America represents for the survival of the United States as a world power.

The discussion of the main sources of controversy between Latin America and the United States that follows is based on the assumption that forthcoming U.S. administrations will again take seriously the idea of a historical or special relationship, and will not break a historical continuity that has so far kept their country safe from aggression from the south. Let us first review the main areas of friction.

**Protection of Private American Interests.** This has been a key element in American foreign policy not only in Latin America, but also in the rest of the world. As former Secretary of State Dean Acheson put it, "For the most part the prewar department was concerned with treaties of commerce or navigation . . . while the general run of business involved extricating Americans from trouble abroad or helping them engage in commercial ventures from which others wished to exclude them."[18]

Yet Latin America is in a process of change, for better or for worse. Nationalism and the struggle for social justice are the main driving forces behind this process. Both imply the possibility of revolutionary or reformist governments clamping down on foreign property for economic or prestige reasons. For the propaganda machinery of authoritarian states the expropriation of foreign property is a windfall. It enhances their prestige and cements their political stability. The fact that the nationalization of a foreign-owned factory or mine will not turn out to be economically profitable does not diminish the political capital it produces. The masses will not be able to measure the loss to their national economy resulting from their government's reckless nationalization policy. In sum, the expropriation of foreign—particularly North American—property is usually rewarding to a Latin American government. Many have tried to profit from it, and many will do so in the future.

That the United States should resort in such cases to retaliation—notably that it should apply the Hickenlooper and González amendments—seems to be a foregone conclusion.[19] How else can it prevent

---

[18] Dean Acheson, *Present at the Creation, My Years in the State Department* (New York: V. W. Norton & Company, 1969), p. 15.

[19] Sec. 620(e) (1) of the Foreign Assistance Act of 1961, as amended, known as the Hickenlooper Amendment, and secs. 21 and 22 of the Inter-American Development Bank Act, known as the González Amendment, call for aid cutoffs in unresolved expropriation disputes. The application of this sanction has been

foreign governments from depriving U.S. citizens of their property? The taking of retaliatory measures may also generate popularity for the chief executive and may, at a given moment, serve as an electoral propaganda tool. Yet a cool assessment of the assets and liabilities of such retaliatory actions might lead to an entirely different conclusion. For such measures, or even an intimation that they might be taken, eventually become a source of irritation and friction between the United States and the Latin American republic affected by them. Such conflicts usually do not remain isolated but reverberate all through the Latin American republics, most of which are favorable sounding boards for complaints about U.S. imperialism.

In other words, the U.S. government should draw a careful balance in every such conflict between the *domestic political* value of protecting its citizens' interests and its own long-term goals and priorities. If bringing pressure to bear upon a Latin American government would seriously damage bilateral relations and inter-American cooperation, it would seem preferable to abstain from retaliation and try to find other ways to compensate the victims of expropriation. It goes without saying that this reasoning contradicts the basic North American concepts of private property, free enterprise, and individual rights. But at this stage in the evolution of Latin America, it is precisely these values that are being hotly contested there, by the radical elites as well as by the populist dictatorships. To defend them rigidly would be to swim against the mainstream of politics in Latin America.

**Human Rights.** Democracy and respect for individual human rights are ingredients of the North American political credo, and the United States is expected to act according to the moral principles professed in its ideology. Paradoxically, there is nothing less rewarding than to champion liberty in a foreign country with a different cultural heritage from one's own. The interpretation of such apparently unequivocal concepts as freedom, democracy, and individual rights can be frustratingly different in a foreign cultural area. We must recognize that there is no universally accepted definition of democracy. To a Marxist-Leninist the word means something quite different from what it means to a Western democrat. For the rightist dictatorship in Latin America, which often stored the most democratic and social constitutions in their national archives, democracy simply meant protecting their country against Communism. U.S. foreign policy makers were unconcerned about the domestic policies of their Latin American partners so long

---

sporadic. For example, in 1968, when the Peruvian military junta nationalized the assets of the International Petroleum Company (a subsidiary of the Standard Oil Company of New Jersey), the U.S. administration refrained from sanctions.

as these protected private American investment, fought domestic Communism, and rallied to the voting pattern of the Western bloc in the United Nations.

Thus, the Carter administration's strong commitment to respect for human rights represents a dramatic change in the U.S. approach to Latin America. And since this is a new beginning we must examine its risks and potential.

No objective analysis of the present Latin American dictatorships can overlook the fact that they are stages in a painful and protracted progress toward a new definition of their own countries' identity. This has followed a cyclical course, with dictatorships and democracies alternating at varying speeds and following varying patterns of conflict. Apparently these countries have so far been unable to assimilate the Western democratic process without resorting to a dialectical interaction of democracy and tyranny. But none has ever established an ideologically based totalitarian regime or destroyed the pillars of their traditional societies—the Church, the military, and private property. It is one of the paradoxes of Latin American history that democracy very often has been reestablished thanks to the intervention of the Church, the military, and the business elite. Does this mean that the dictatorships that presently rule most of South America will yield again to democratic governments within less than a generation? This question is open to discussion today, although it has happened at various times in Latin American history.

The coups d'etat that brought military juntas to power in several Latin American countries in the postwar era cannot be justified on moral grounds. Yet they were preceded by events that set the stage for them. Democratic governments failed to fulfill the expectations vested in them by their constituents. As the economic boom that immediately followed World War II gradually receded, a protracted economic crisis began to stifle progress and increase poverty in the area. The impoverished middle classes gave birth to rural and city guerrilla movements that undermined political stability and aggravated the crisis in the economy. It was this that underlay the emergence of military dictatorships in Brazil, Bolivia, Peru, and Uruguay. The Allende government in Chile failed to consolidate its slim electoral victory and sharpened the conflict with the Christian Democratic and Conservative opposition, thus leading the country into an impasse. In Argentina the polarization of the Peronista party and the ineptitude of the aging former dictator and his widow-successor paved the way for a military takeover. And it should be added that in the Andean countries in particular, and in Brazil and the southern cone of South America to a lesser extent, the low degree of political participation has rendered democracy illusory, since democratic games are still being played largely within the preserves of the ruling elites.

In order to qualify correctly the military dictatorships in South America in the 1970s, one must keep in mind that, with the exception of Paraguay, they are the collective enterprises of the military establishment rather than one-man tyrannies in the *caudillo* tradition. They are also development-oriented and economically, or in the case of Peru socially, progressive. Despite all the errors and bungling that have characterized the Brazilian and Peruvian military juntas, the fact remains that the former was responsible for the Brazilian economic miracle, and the latter for the first non-Communist socialist system in Latin America. The Chilean and Uruguayan dictatorships have existed for too short a time to permit an evaluation of their potential.

Can such achievements or hopes of achievement justify the existence of torture chambers and prison camps for political dissidents? It would be both cynical and immoral to answer in the affirmative. President Carter's policy of reserving U.S. aid for nations that respect human rights is in line with the noblest ideals of the North American heritage, but the success of his policy hinges on a number of factors.

First of all, a policy on human rights must be consistent; that is, it should not deny aid to Latin American countries that trample human rights under foot while continuing to extend it to strategically more sensitive areas (South Korea, for example). There is nothing more self-defeating than to apply a moral principle selectively.

The U.S. stance on human rights can only be effective if it reaches the Latin American masses. Otherwise, it will run into the same syndrome of ills that brought down the Alliance for Progress, which alienated the rulers without winning over the ruled. The military and business elites that benefit from stability under dictatorship are loath to reopen the valves of public opinion to let out the steam of discontent. The underprivileged masses tend to be ignorant of politics, and can easily be manipulated by government propaganda. Their main problem is an economic one. As four-time president of Ecuador José M. Velasco Ibarra observed: "While man remains a slave to his material needs, to his illnesses, to his ignorance and vices, he cannot be free. A merely external, formal, and legal freedom is nothing but a lie."[20] Besides the upper classes, considerable numbers of the middle class also benefit from the economic policy of the Latin American military regimes, and are therefore indifferent to human rights. On the other hand, the poorer

---

[20] José M. Velasco Ibarra, *Caos politico en el mundo contemporaneo* (Guayaquil, Ecuador: Editorial Royal Print, 1964), p. 131.

echelons of the middle class are usually so imbued with leftist propaganda that they are skeptical and mistrustful of any policy promoted by the United States. President Carter's inclusion of social justice among human rights therefore represents a valuable addition to American propaganda.

A human rights policy tied to retaliation in the area of military aid may bring about a shift in the Latin American military dictatorships' orientation in foreign policy. The U.S.S.R. and its allies are not squeamish in their choice of trade partners and allies. While on the surface more ideologically oriented than the West, they are in fact hard pragmatists motivated by their ambition for power. But a dramatic about-face like Cuba's in the early 1960s is unlikely to take place, simply because the Soviet Union is unable to shoulder the economic, financial, and military tasks that fall to the United States in regard to Latin America. But even sporadic penetration by Soviet military influence could create fissures in the hemispheric defense system that must be avoided.

Last but not least, a human rights policy must not raise the specter of U.S. paternalism or of a big stick. This would be entirely counterproductive and a windfall for the dictatorships.

Any decent person can only wish for the success of President Carter's human rights policy in Latin America and elsewhere in the world. But the path to success in this undertaking is studded with roadblocks and pitfalls, and it requires the skill of a tightrope walker to travel along it.

### The Panama Canal Treaties of September 1977

On September 6, 1977, the Presidents of the United States and Panama signed three agreements in Washington: the Panama Canal Treaty, the Treaty Concerning the Permanent Neutrality and Operation of the Panama Canal, and the Protocol to the Treaty Concerning the Permanent Neutrality and Operation of the Panama Canal.[21] These legal accords supersede the Hay–Bunau-Varilla Treaty of 1903 and all other treaties, conventions, agreements, and exchanges of notes between the United States and the Republic of Panama concerning the Panama Canal (Panama Canal Treaty, Article I, pars. (a), (b), and (c)).

The 1903 treaty gave the United States an imprecisely defined jurisdiction over the Canal Zone and allowed Panama to hold "residual sovereignty" over this territory. The interpretation of this concept has

---

[21] Quotations from the treaties were taken from a special supplement to the September 7, 1977 issue of the *New York Times*.

changed several times since the Republic of Panama was created more than seven decades ago. The 1936 treaty of friendship and cooperation between the United States and Panama defined the Canal Zone as a "territory of Panama under U.S. jurisdiction." The Eisenhower-Remon treaty in 1955 reverted to the concept of greater U.S. sovereignty. The Kissinger-Tack agreement of February 7, 1974, stipulated the gradual abrogation of the Hay–Bunau-Varilla treaty and the phasing out of the attributes of U.S. sovereignty. The new Panama Canal Treaty is based largely on the principles of this provisory agreement. It recognizes *ex nunc* Panama's territorial sovereignty over the Canal Zone, but partially suspends the rights stemming from them until December 31, 1999. In this context Article I, paragraph 2, stipulates that "the Republic of Panama, as *territorial sovereign* (emphasis added), grants to the United States of America, for the duration of this treaty, the rights necessary to regulate the transit of ships through the Panama Canal, and to manage, improve, protect and defend the Canal." By the year 2000 Panama will recover full jurisdiction over the Canal Zone and, of course, the canal itself. But even during the years before 2000 it is agreed that "the Republic of Panama shall increasingly participate in the management and protection and defense of the Canal as provided by this Treaty" (Article I, paragraph 3).

Panamanian cooperation with the United States in the management of the canal will be coordinated by the new Panama Canal Commission. Its board will be composed of nine members; five U.S. nationals, and four Panamanian nationals selected by the Republic of Panama but appointed by the United States (Article III, paragraph 3). Although the Panama Canal Treaty and its annex provide a fairly detailed description of the rights and duties of the Panama Canal Commission as an agency of the United States, the outlook for U.S.-Panamanian cooperation within and outside of this agency is studded with possible problems. Paragraph 10 of Article III provides, for example, that Panama will seek from its legislature such legislation as may be needed to guarantee the security of the Panama Canal Commission, its property, its employees, and so forth. Yet, there is no assurance that future Panamanian governments will indeed comply with this commitment or that the United States could enforce its implementation.

Another area of possible friction is Article XI of the treaty, which states that, for thirty calendar months following the effective date of the treaty, the criminal and civil laws of the United States will apply concurrently with those of the Republic of Panama. After this transition period the Republic of Panama will reassume plenary jurisdiction over the former Canal Zone, except in criminal cases relating to offenses committed in violation of laws prior to the date of the treaty (Article XI, paragraph 3).

Unfortunately, Article XIV of the Panama Canal Treaty, which concerns the settlement of disputes, is couched in imprecise terms that hardly provide firm legal guidelines for solving the problems. It is left up to the good will of the contracting parties to resolve the matter "through consultation in the appropriate committees" or "through diplomatic channels." Both sides may also "agree to submit the matter to conciliation, mediation, arbitration, or such other procedure for the peaceful settlement of the dispute as they may mutually deem appropriate." Since there is no inter-American court for the settlement of legal disputes between American nations, it is difficult to see to what kind of authority the U.S. and Panama will eventually turn for conciliation or arbitration of disputes.

The greatest challenge to U.S.-Panamanian cooperation could arise in the event of a shift in Panamanian politics toward an alliance with a power or powers hostile to the United States. The Panama Canal Treaty reserves for the United States "primary responsibility to protect and defend the Canal" (Article IV, paragraph 2) during the period covered by the treaty. It also stipulates that the United States will have the right to station, train, and move military forces within the Republic of Panama. A combined board composed of an equal number of senior military representatives of the United States and Panama will survey and coordinate all operations pertaining to the protection and defense of the canal (Article IV, paragraph 3).

Article IV, paragraph 2, thus underscores the fact that in matters of defense the sovereign rights of Panama are restricted, and the United States has responsibility for protecting the canal against threats of armed attack by a third party. It is also presumable that the American right and duty to defend the canal extends to cases of political subversion or the threat of guerrilla warfare, although this is not expressly stated in the treaty.

But the question remains: Who will defend the canal after the termination of the treaty in the year 2000? The Treaty Concerning the Permanent Neutrality and Operation of the Panama Canal stipulates that the canal will remain permanently neutral (Article IV), while the Republic of Panama "shall operate the canal and maintain military forces, defense sites and military installations within its national territory" (Article V). Nevertheless, Article VI of the Neutrality Treaty stipulates that U.S. and Panamanian vessels of war are entitled to transit the canal *expeditiously* [emphasis added]. North American critics find this formulation ambiguous with regard to safeguarding U.S. interests, while Panamanian critics consider it an infraction of the principle of permanent neutrality of the canal.

Article IV of the Neutrality Treaty suggests that the United States and Panama are to be joint guarantors of the canal's neutrality. ("The United States and the Republic of Panama agree to maintain the regime of neutrality established in this Treaty. . . .") Yet, this was one of the aspects of the treaties which drew criticism from the public and Congress. President Carter thus deemed it necessary to make another clarification. On October 14, 1977, he invited the President of Panama, General Omar Torrijos, to visit Washington and discuss again the issue of American rights to protect the canal's neutrality after the expiration of the treaty. They issued a joint communique after their meeting which stated, *inter alia*: "Under the treaty concerning the permanent neutrality and operation of the Panama Canal, Panama and the United States have the responsibility to assure that the Panama Canal will remain open and secure to ships of all nations."[22]

Obviously, the entire legal framework of these treaties relies on the assumption that the United States and Panama are allies, and that their bona fide cooperation cannot be disrupted by disputes over the interpretation of individual clauses of the treaties. The United States and Panama, it is therefore assumed, will defend the neutrality of the canal and are ready to defend it jointly against any kind of aggression. This assumption is based on the fact that the major world powers view Central America as a sphere of North American influence. In twenty years or so, however, the balance of forces might be radically altered by the emergence of a leftist Latin American alliance endorsed by the Soviet Union. The Isthmus of Panama may then become the hub of a new power system. The treaty does not indicate the likely U.S. position in the event of that development.

A considerable part of the criticism expressed by retired U.S. generals, admirals, and other former commanders claims that the treaties are a sign of American withdrawal, that would, in turn, lead to a power vacuum in the Caribbean which the Soviet Union and Cuba may exploit. We will later deal with the arguments of the U.S. military, and will examine them together with the theses of those who view the canal as vital to U.S. commerce.

The strongest opposition to the treaties is voiced by a part of the American public which fears the loss of U.S. prestige and condemns the give-away of American property. Some of their arguments lack a rational and pragmatic analysis of the advantages and possible pitfalls of the treaties. At the same time, advocates of the treaty note that

---

[22] *International Herald Tribune*, October 17, 1977.

American withdrawal from a colonial position is a historic necessity. The West European nations relinquished their colonial empires after World War II, when colonialism, except in the view of the Soviet Union, ceased to be a morally and legally justifiable basis for the relationship between a major power and a small country. The United States created the artificial state of Panama as a virtual dependency in 1902 and converted the Panama Canal Zone into an American colony. This is still a negative factor in U.S.-Latin American relations. No inter-American meeting in recent years failed to attack the terms of the old U.S.-Panamanian treaty. Not only Panama demands the abolition of the colonial status of the isthmus; other Latin American republics do so with almost equal fervor and determination. In 1973, for example, the Latin American delegates to the United Nations, in resounding demonstration of solidarity and identification with Panama, took the unprecedented step of reelecting Panama to the UN Security Council only two years after the expiration of its previous term.

Panamanian nationalists criticize the terms of the treaties providing for a twenty-two-year delay in the establishment of full Panamanian sovereignty over the Canal Zone. Vocal opposition forces in Panama campaigned against the ratification of the treaties, maintaining that the neutrality treaty will allow the United States to intervene in Panamanian domestic affairs, that the canal is not neutral as long as preference is given to U.S. warships and, finally, that the treaties might strengthen and perpetuate military rule in Panama.[23]

Fortunately, the referendum held on the treaties in Panama on October 23, 1977, resulted in a comfortable victory for Torrijos. Out of a total of 765,659 votes cast, 506,927 voted for and 245,112 voted against the treaties, in the largest voter turnout in Panamanian history.[24]

It is therefore up to the U.S. Senate to give its consent to the ratification of the treaties. At present, the dispute over the right of the United States to protect the neutrality of the canal continues, but regardless of the Senate's decision, it is important to analyze the pros and cons of the treaty and its meaning for the future.

The economic importance of the Panama Canal for the United States is considerable, but not vital. Seventeen percent of U.S. oceanborne commerce passes through it. The interchange of East Coast coal and West Coast oil, for example, takes place through the canal. Yet, loss of this waterway would affect only 1 percent of the U.S. gross national product. Its relative narrowness prevents the canal from accommodating large modern oil tankers, let alone aircraft carriers.

---

[23] Marlise Simons in the *Washington Post*, October 13, 1977.
[24] UPI dispatch from Panama, October 29, 1977.

The relative economic importance of the canal is far greater for at least nine Latin American nations than it is for the United States. Thirty percent of Panama's GNP is derived from the canal and the zone, 75 percent of the canal's employees are Panamanians, and the level of U.S. aid to Panama is higher per capita than to any other country in the world. Nicaragua ships 76.8 percent of its cargoes through the canal; El Salvador, 66.4 percent; Ecuador, Peru, Colombia, and Chile, between 30 and 51 percent.[25] But shipping through the canal is also important to a number of Eastern and Southeast Asian countries like Japan, Vietnam, Taiwan, and Korea, as well as New Zealand.

The strategic value of the canal is open to discussion. Owing to its vulnerability to missiles or strategic bombers, it would be of little value in the event of a global nuclear war. Yet in a local or regional armed conflict, this waterway might acquire considerable importance for the United States. During the Korean and Vietnam wars, for example, 95 percent of all military cargoes were carried by ship. As a result, the transit of U.S. public vessels through the canal doubled and quintupled, respectively, during those conflicts.[26] But this concerns only cargo vessels. U.S. naval strategy is essentially based on a two-ocean-navy concept, although nuclear submarines can, for example, pass through the canal.

The canal and the zone are also extremely vulnerable to subversion and guerrilla warfare. They can only be protected if the hinterland is safe; that is, if Panama stands with the United States. If Panama is hostile it can close the canal to American shipping. The United States might then be forced to a Suez-type recapture, one expert suggests, and that would administer a final blow to the inter-American system.[27]

Let us examine this question in light of what happened to the Suez Canal in 1965. The closing of that waterway lasted almost twenty years, and did far more damage to the host country, Egypt, than to the powerful Western shipping companies, which were able to adjust their navigation pattern and route their ships around the Cape of Good Hope. As noted above, the Panama Canal is vitally important to the Republic of Panama, something that can hardly be said about the Suez Canal in relation to Egypt. Thus, the government of Panama should be reluctant to undertake any unprovoked action that would expose the

---

[25] Thomas M. Franck and Edward Weisban, "Panama Paralysis," *Foreign Policy*, no. 21 (Winter 1975–1976), p. 179, fn. 6.
[26] Charles Mechling Jr., "The Panama Canal: A Fresh Start," *ORBIS*, vol. 20, no. 4 (Winter 1977), p. 1013.
[27] Ibid., p. 1022. See also Robert G. Cox, "Choices for Partnership or Bloodshed in Panama," in *Americas in a Changing World*, pp. 138-141.

canal to destructive military operations—so long as its pride as a sovereign nation is respected.

In conclusion, the concessions made by the United States in the treaties were a political necessity, a price it had to pay in order to secure future cooperation with Latin America. Thus, in the long run, U.S. hemispheric security aims are served better by the treaties than by a garrison of soldiers in the Isthmus of Panama. Some details of the treaties are open to criticism, but their underlying concept, namely, the surrender of a relic of North American colonial history in favor of greater Latin American cooperation and good will, appears to be a step in the right direction.

For reasons of security it might be desirable to encourage other Latin American states to participate in the defense of the canal. An attempt in this direction has been made in Article VII, paragraph 1, of the Neutrality Treaty, which provides that the United States of America and the Republic of Panama will "jointly sponsor a resolution in the Organization of American States opening to accession by all states of the world the protocol to this treaty."

This article and the protocol to the Neutrality Treaty, if used, add a new dimension to the treaties.

## The Special Relationship Concept

For a number of reasons already explained, the author believes in continuation of the close historical relationship between the two Americas. But a new approach to this relationship would require dismantling the remnants of paternalism bequeathed by Manifest Destiny and the Monroe Doctrine. The new "mature partnership" often emphasized by recent U.S. administrations could be based on the following, tentative premises:

(1) reaffirming the nonintervention principle, including recognition of the political pluralism of Latin America—that is, a sort of anti-Brezhnev Doctrine that would counter the neocolonial approach of the U.S.S.R. to its satellites with an American doctrine of tolerance;

(2) restructuring the OAS into a bipolar organization in which the Latin American community would have special rights and responsibilities;

(3) strengthening the hemispheric security system against outside aggression, either by refining and amplifying the provisions of the Rio Treaty or by joining the Latin American community of nations in an organization along the lines of NATO; and

(4) as a quid pro quo for a stronger security system, making

generous U.S. trade concessions, abolishing many of the present restrictions, and establishing a preferential customs pattern.

The United States and Latin America are interdependent in their trade, security, and cultural needs. But their present pattern of relations is outdated and ineffective, and frought with a long-run security risk for the United States. One of the most prominent North American students of Latin American-U.S. relations wrote recently: "The spread of Third World myth in Latin America has just about completed the dissipation of that other myth, the Western Hemisphere idea."[28] Yet, myths do not die quickly; they are deeply rooted in the psyche of the peoples who generated them. Chile might be farther from the United States than Portugal, but it is closer in terms of common historical heritage and a common sensibility to hemispheric developments. For that dream of a new world, where men are equal and free, and where their ambition and creative stimuli are not bridled by the rigid structures and timeworn traditions of the old world, still survives in the minds of all Americans, both to the North and to the South of the Rio Grande. The vitality of this American spirit remains a source of energy, which might bind together or separate the two Americas, depending on how leaders to the North and to the South will use it.

At the present stage the United States is still free to choose between infusing new life into the Western Hemisphere idea by reconstructing its juridical and political framework, or to let Latin America drift toward the new horizons of a vaguely defined Third World alignment.

---

[28] Arthur P. Whitaker, "America in the Western Hemisphere," *ORBIS*, vol. 20, no. 1 (Spring 1976), p. 177.